C000010093

THE HAMMERS

THE HAMMERS
The West Ham United Dream Team

JASON TOMAS

MAINSTREAM
PUBLISHING

EDINBURGH AND LONDON

Copyright © Jason Tomas 1997
All rights reserved
The moral right of the author has been asserted

First published in Great Britain in 1997 by
MAINSTREAM PUBLISHING COMPANY (EDINBURGH) LTD
7 Albany Street
Edinburgh EH1 3UG

ISBN 1 85158 928 7

No part of this book may be reproduced or transmitted in any form or by
any means without written permission from the publisher, except by a
reviewer who wishes to quote brief passages in connection with a review
written for insertion in a magazine, newspaper or broadcast

Photographs courtesy of Steve Bacon and Recorder Newspapers

A catalogue record for this book is available from the British Library

Printed and bound in Great Britain by Butler and Tanner Ltd

Contents

	Introduction	7
1	Bobby Moore, Martin Peters and Geoff Hurst	11
2	Bobby Moore, Martin Peters and Geoff Hurst	37
3	Billy Bonds	53
4	Phil Parkes	69
5	Alvin Martin	83
6	Rio Ferdinand	99
7	Julian Dicks	111
8	Trevor Brooking and Alan Devonshire	123
9	Ronnie Boyce	147
10	The Manager and Substitutes	161

Introduction

Football, it is said, is a game of opinions.

The managers of national teams will all confirm that, if they were to take heed of every opinion concerning the players they should select for their starting line-ups – from fellow professionals, the media and the fans – they could easily end up with a mind-boggling array of different sides.

However, when it comes to choosing a West Ham dream team from all the top-class players who have worn that claret and light-blue jersey since the war, there cannot be many arguments against the XI I have chosen – can there?

Bearing in mind West Ham's reputation as one of the most advanced clubs in British football, in terms of their coaching expertise and awareness of tactical developments, the players selected would have no problems at all in forming themselves into a modern-day shape. That shape is 3-5-1-1 (note the use of three central defenders and just one front man) and the team is:

PHIL PARKES

ALVIN MARTIN   BOBBY MOORE   RIO FERDINAND

BILLY BONDS   JULIAN DICKS

TREVOR BROOKING   RONNIE BOYCE   ALAN DEVONSHIRE

MARTIN PETERS

GEOFF HURST

And, waiting in the wings to come into it – from the substitutes' bench – are Ken Brown, Frank Lampard, Harry Redknapp, Johnny Byrne and Frank McAvennie.

One who has no real arguments against the line-up is Dave Thomas, a *Sunday Times* writer and self-confessed West Ham 'addict', who has helped in the research and writing of this book. The team also gets the thumbs up from Trevor Smith, a man who has seen more West Ham matches than the rest of us have had hot dinners.

The 64-year-old Smith, the sports editor of the *Ilford and Newham Recorder* newspaper, has been covering the Hammers for the last 40 years. He initially joined the group in 1949 and it was largely as a result of his initiative that they started focusing their attention on West Ham United FC in the mid-1950s. 'Until then,' he recalls, 'most of the football interest was centred on the success of the area's famous amateur team, Ilford, who won the FA Amateur Cup two seasons in succession. But by the time I finished my National Service in the RAF in 1953, amateur football was dying on its feet and it seemed to me that, in terms of our soccer coverage, West Ham was where our future was.'

Smith, born and raised in east London, had already established links with the club through his family. He explains: 'My maternal grandfather delivered coal to most of the West Ham players, and, as a boy, my father ran errands for Charlie Paynter [West Ham's manager from 1932 to 1950].' In his own case, Smith, a West Ham fan as a boy, played for the same school house team as the son of Ted Fenton [the Hammers' manager from 1950 to 1956] and with and against a number of West Ham's stars of the 1950s in youth football.

It is partly for this reason that Smith singles out West Ham's 1957–58 Second Division promotion-winning side as the one that has given him the most pleasure. He says: 'You have to remember that I knew a lot of those players personally – they were of the same generation as me – and I harboured the same dreams of playing for West Ham that they did.

'I used to play at outside-left for a team in a local youth league, and I always remember a friendly match against a side called Neville United, which was made up of lads from Neville Road [a street renowned in east London as a fertile breeding ground for professional footballers]. The manager said to me: "Look, I'd like to try a few things for this game – you play at centre-half. There is no need to worry about it because Neville United are going to be experimenting, too; they will be playing their centre-half at centre-forward." That player scored a hat-trick against me in the first half and his name was Ken Brown.'

The same Ken Brown who went on to help steer West Ham to that Second Division Championship triumph in 1958.

'My association with players like Ken was not the only reason why I felt a particular affinity with that team,' Smith adds. 'West Ham had previously been in the Second Division for 26 years and a lot of their fans felt that the club lacked ambition. The general feeling was that West Ham were quite content to be where they were. This was why my father stopped going to watch them.'

Another West Ham team which gave Smith particular satisfaction was the Hammers side who reached the 1965 European Cup-Winners' Cup final. Interestingly, when you ask him to pinpoint the most stirring West Ham match he has ever seen, he plumps not for the Wembley win over TSV Munich 1860, but the 1–1 draw with Real Zaragoza in the semi-final second-leg tie in Spain. 'Real, who had lost the first leg 2–1, kicked lumps out of us in that return match, and when they took the lead I don't think anyone felt that West Ham could survive,' he recalls. 'Of all the great West Ham performances I have seen, that was the one that stands out in my memory the most.'

His favourite West Ham player? He has to think even longer about that one but eventually singles out Alan Devonshire. 'He was probably the one who surprised me the most,' he says. 'He joined West Ham from non-league football, and only cost £5,000. He'd been rejected by Malcolm Allison at Crystal Palace and, as Malcolm was so well respected among the Hammers fans (having once been one of their favourite players), I think the general reaction to Devonshire was that he couldn't possibly be that good. As it turned out, he was a revelation, wasn't he? Oh, none of the West Ham players I have watched had greater attacking flair than he did.'

Needless to say, Smith is immediately encouraged by the selection of Devonshire in this West Ham fantasy team. As for the other choices, he says: 'I could possibly make one or two changes. But by and large it looks a very good team.'

Hopefully, you will feel the same when you've read this book . . .

CHAPTER 1

Bobby Moore, Martin Peters and Geoff Hurst

Bobby Moore, Martin Peters and Geoff Hurst. A defender, an all-purpose player and a centre-forward – and surely, the very first names on anyone's team sheet for a West Ham dream XI.

How could it be otherwise when, if one were to compile a similar fantasy football line-up for an England side, the Hammers trio – arguably the key playing figures behind the 1966 World Cup triumph under Sir Alf Ramsey's management – could stake particularly strong claims for automatic places in that side, too? Millions of words have been expounded on the abilities of Moore, Peters and Hurst, but as far as their long connection with West Ham is concerned, the most authoritative voices on the subject are those of Ron Greenwood and John Lyall.

Greenwood was West Ham's manager for almost all of their long careers at the club, while Lyall, prior to succeeding Greenwood as manager in 1974, experienced a similarly close association with them in his roles as coach and assistant manager. Not surprisingly, that association provided the most intriguing aspect of the books that Greenwood and Lyall once wrote about their own careers. Unlike Greenwood, Lyall, who initially joined West Ham as a full-back but whose professional career was restricted to just three years because of injury problems, had the distinction of being a playing colleague of the

11

trio when they, too, were taking their first steps in the game. In his book *Just Like My Dreams*, written in collaboration with Michael Hart and published in 1989, he wrote:

As a trio with one club, they were unique. They were players with skill and intellect. They were quite superb. They acknowledged their fame and glory in a self-effacing manner, though there were times, when the team were playing particularly well, when they became a little boisterous. On one such occasion, we were preparing for a difficult game at Leeds and I felt I needed to bring them down to earth a little bit.

Ron had left me in charge of training that day, and I devised a routine that was difficult, but probably just within their capabilities. If they failed to do it, I would have made a little point – none of us are perfect, lads – but if they succeeded, I would have to hold up my hands in admiration. I used the entire length of a training pitch at Chadwell Heath with a goalkeeper at one end and Hurst, Moore and Peters strung across the width of the pitch at the other. They had to pass the ball between them as they worked the ball the length of the field and then score. The catch was that the ball wasn't allowed to touch the ground at any stage and each player, on receiving, had only one touch. In other words, they had to volley or head their passes between them from one goal to the other, using the width of the pitch. Most of the other team members were on the sidelines speculating about the degree of difficulty and who was most likely to fail among these three great players. None did, and I held my hands up in admiration.

I arrived as a youngster at West Ham [in 1957] a year before Bobby and, although it was plain to see he had enormous potential, you simply couldn't envisage the sort of career that was to follow for him.

We were great pals. As teenagers together, we young lads used to go dancing in our shiny mohair suits at the Ilford Palais, and Bobby, as immaculate as ever, always looked a little cut above everyone else.

If we were out late, I often stayed with Bobby at his parents' house in Barking. No matter what time we arrived home, he always carefully brushed down his suit before he went to bed. He was just as fastidious as a player. Albert Walker [West Ham's team attendant] used to give each first-team player a pair of tie-ups for his socks before the first match of the season. Most players, when they returned to the dressing-room after the match, would throw them into a muddy pile and expect another pair before the next home game. Not Bobby! He picked the mud off the tie-ups, folded them neatly, and tucked them into his boots. At the end of each season, he had the same pair of tie-ups he started with.

He was just as careful about tucking a clean white handkerchief into his shorts before every game. Those little things illustrate how diligently he looked after the details in his life. He devoted the same detail to his game.

As a player, he had immense foresight, vision and knowledge. He had an enquiring mind, and what he learned, particularly from Ron, helped make him one of the great international captains. He liked to play the game properly and he led both England and West Ham by example. He could see and interpret correctly everything that was happening on the pitch. That's what gave him such wonderful vision. He was always looking for the space to play the ball into. If he couldn't see it in front of him or on the wings, he was happy to play the ball back to his own goalkeeper, knowing this would draw the opposition out of their defensive positions and create space for West Ham's attackers.

He was also a great interceptor, one of the best I have ever seen in the game. He didn't have to tackle very often because he invariably knew where the ball was going and he would be there first.

With such a man, it was no surprise that he went on to captain England in the World Cup final victory over West Germany and win 108 international caps.

As a young coach, I appreciated the way he helped make my task easier. I remember being put in charge of the team for a foreign trip for the first time in May 1971. I was assistant manager, and the club had agreed to go on an 11-match four-week tour of the United States. Ron knew he would be busy in London that summer, so he asked me to take charge, he felt it would be good experience for me. It was no easy task for the players at the end of a long season – particularly for Bobby, who had spent the previous summer at the World Cup finals in Mexico and most of the summers before that on duty with England. I took all the senior players, including Geoff Hurst, another uncomplaining England workhorse who would probably have preferred a rest.

Soon after we arrived in the States, Bobby came to me and said: 'John, do whatever you want. I'll play every game if you want. Don't feel you have to substitute me either, unless you want to do it for tactical reasons.' He played all 11 games for me. I sensed that he wanted to help me make a success of my career. The other lads felt the same way. It was all part of the family atmosphere at Upton Park.

Despite world-wide fame, Bobby was an unassuming man. Those who don't know him have suggested he is aloof but nothing could be further from the truth. As a player at West Ham, he wanted to be treated like all the others, and would often put his team-mates before himself. I remember on that trip to the States, standing in the bar of a Los Angeles hotel with Bobby and the entire first-team squad. I had given the players a couple of days off between matches, and they were enjoying a quiet, relaxing evening. At the end of the evening the waiter produced the bill for the drinks, and Bobby took it quietly and said: 'I'll pay.' I told him it wasn't necessary because all the lads were receiving a daily spending allowance, but he insisted.

When he retired from playing, I was surprised that he did not pursue a managerial career more vigorously, because he had the experience, temperament, knowledge and love of the game that is required in management. But perhaps players of Bobby's status can diversify when they retire and don't need to devote their time to management.

Geoff Hurst was from a similar mould. The way he responded in training gave me enormous confidence.

He came to West Ham [in 1959] as a wing-half from Chelmsford and, at that stage, you could never imagine him rewriting the history books with a hat-trick in the World Cup final. He was a powerful, confident lad, a good all-round sportsman who played County cricket for Essex. When he was a wing-half in West Ham's reserves, we played a number of games together. He never looked comfortable in that role. But he had excellent technique for such a big man, and his raw strength gave a competitive edge to his game. Ron obviously realised we were not getting the best out of him, and decided to try him as a central striker alongside Johnny Byrne [who had been bought from Crystal Palace for £65,000 in March 1962].

Determination and aggression were the qualities that underpinned Geoff's game. He wanted to succeed, and he worked as hard as Bobby on the training ground. He developed into an outstanding, very coachable striker, who Ron, in later years as England manager, used to demonstrate skills and tactics to his international stars. There are few players of 6ft who can be both physically commanding and possess superb technique. Geoff had both qualities. His years as a wing-half had taught him the value of mobility, and this made him an unselfish team player. He would run wide to create space for others or, with his back to goal, would draw team-mates into the play. And, when facing goal, his pace, power and courage took him into the most difficult situations.

He was the outstanding all-round striker of his era, and would be priceless in the modern age, when strikers are basically pigeon-holed in two categories. They are either the target man or the goalscorer who feeds off him. Geoff could fill both roles.

Martin Peters [who joined West Ham as an apprentice in

1959 and has become a close friend and business colleague of Hurst] was as talented as any player I have seen, and his determination to succeed was fuelled by a deep love of the game. As a young player, he would be the first to arrive at the training ground and then implore any other early starters to work with him out on the pitch before the organised training began.

I remember one Friday morning at Upton Park, watching him and Harry Redknapp playing about together. Harry was crossing from the corner flag and Martin was almost lazily volleying the ball into the back of the net. It was something that came naturally to him. As I watched them, I heard Martin shout to Harry: 'Chip one in, and I'll hit the crossbar.' Harry centred the ball and Martin drove his shot, first time, smack against the crossbar.

'Lucky,' Harry shouted.

Martin just smiled.

'I bet you five-to-one you can't do it again,' cried Harry, who enjoyed a little wager occasionally.

Martin accepted, and when the ball came over – a perfect centre to be fair to Harry – Martin drove it, first time, smack against the crossbar. By this time Harry was a little perplexed, not to mention concerned about his money.

'Double or nothing,' he shouted. Again Martin accepted. Again the ball came across, falling nicely in front of him, waist-high, and Martin volleyed it straight against the crossbar – three times out of three.

He was a very special player with a very special talent. The fact that he wore every shirt for West Ham, from the goalkeeper's jersey to number 11, illustrated his immense versatility. He was a European type of player, comfortable and secure in any position.

But even Peters, the natural thoroughbred among this great soccer triumvirate, needed someone to direct his ability through the right channels. For Peters, and also Moore and Hurst, that is where Ron Greenwood came in.

Greenwood, who came to West Ham in 1961 after a spell as first-team coach at Arsenal, was without doubt one of the most talented coaches British football has ever produced. It was during his 13-year reign at Upton Park that West Ham truly established their image as an academy of advanced soccer skills. Indeed, in both his manner and his deep-thinking approach to the game, Greenwood was more like a professor than a football manager. In that respect, though he could appear irritatingly arrogant and dictatorial, especially to established stars, Moore, Hurst and Peters could justifiably claim to be the pupils who benefitted from him the most.

In his book *Sincerely Yours*, written in collaboration with Bryon Butler and published in 1974, Greenwood put it this way:

> All three were waiting for me when I joined West Ham, young chaps waiting to be taken in hand. I cannot say I anticipated much success when I inherited the trio. Peters was the gifted one. His talent stood out like a chapel hat peg, but he was still in the youth team. Moore was a first-class technician and a quick learner, but he was heavy-legged, not a good runner and a poor header. His promise seemed limited. Hurst was just a big, strong ordinary wing-half, happy when going forward but a terrible defender. The raw talent was all there, but the shaping and maturing of it took time.
>
> There was even doubt about their best positions. Moore's climb to distinction began after I switched him from wing-half to central defence. Hurst only became a player when I moved him into attack. Peters was so versatile, he wore every shirt from one to eleven and had to ask me: 'What is my best position?' At that moment, I did not know.

Here's how Greenwood explained the development of the players.

> Moore had won his spurs as West Ham's left-half by the time I joined them at the end of the 1960–61 season although, curiously, he had been dropped a couple of times by Mr

Pratt, the chairman, and Phil Woosnam, who ran the side between Ted Fenton's departure and my arrival. Hurst had got their nod instead and Moore, mortally hurt as only youngsters can be, soon came to see me.

I understood his attitude; pride is part of a good player's make-up. He said he was worried about his future, but I told him his future was West Ham's future. 'I've known you some time, in the England Youth and Under-23 teams [of which Greenwood was the manager], and I feel we can build this club around you,' I told him. I was not flattering him. I meant it.

There was always something about Moore. He looked good, of course; nice height and strong build, blond hair, determined chin and cool, knowing eyes. He did not win any major acclaim as a schoolboy and, in fact, showed more promise as a cricketer. But once he started to move, there was no stopping him.

I first spotted him playing in a schoolboys' match at Stamford Bridge. I was impressed by his presence and solidness on the ball and, although West Ham saw him as a wing-half, I used him in central defence as soon as we got together with England's Youth team. He began playing centre-half for West Ham's reserves, though not with much success. A lot of goals went past him because he wasn't sure of himself in the air. I was manager at Eastbourne at the time, but Geoff Hurst remembers how other players at Upton Park used to gripe about their number five. They all said much the same thing: 'Get Moore out of that position.' They got their way and Moore switched back to left-half, but this did not worry me because my youth team played a lot of Continental sides who tended to keep the ball on the ground. Moore coped splendidly with them.

There was no sign yet, however, that Moore was going to become a player of world stature. He looked as if he might be very good, but there were a lot of better-equipped youngsters about. He did not have much pace, or even variety in the pace he had, and there were people around who would say that he couldn't cope with a 'chasing'. Moore's critics could see that he had weaknesses, and certainly he did not have the natural talent of Martin Peters. But what few people knew about was his fanatical dedication.

Moore made himself into a great player. I rarely had a conversation with young Moore. He simply asked questions. He wanted to know everything. He would quiz me for hours, just picking my brain, and I was delighted to oblige. He would slip into the seat next to me, on a plane or coach, and in a professional sense we became very close. We talked for hours and, during practice and in games, I could see it was time well spent.

I studied Real Madrid in one match and told Moore how their full-backs played early balls down the line with the outside of the front foot so that their intentions were disguised. He mastered the technique – front foot, outside contact, early ball to target already in mind – and used it throughout his career. His front foot was always his right.

There were times when I was deliberately unkind to Moore. I even told him he would never win a place in Hartlepool's side because he couldn't head the ball. But he got round that problem, too. He would use his mind and feet to get into exactly the right position, so that he could let the ball drop and take it with his chest or foot. He was difficult to fault, he was a perfectionist.

Moore's switch from left-half to central defence came in my first full season. We were playing Leicester, an intelligent, well co-ordinated side, and to counter one or two things I knew they would try, I suggested a new role to Bobby. 'Drop back – play deeper and play loose,' I told him. He slotted into the role beautifully, working alongside and to the left of Ken Brown at centre-half. That gave our full-backs the chance to go in and get closer to their opponents, and the balance of the side improved immediately. Bobby had found his niche.

His international chance came suddenly in 1962. England reached the finals of the World Cup in Chile and Walter Winterbottom, the team manager, named his squad early.

Not so long before before departure, though, he told me he thought he had a wing-half problem and my reply was immediate. 'Why not take Bobby Moore? He won't let you down.' We had often talked about Moore and such a strong recommendation didn't surprise Winterbottom; he probably half-expected it. Moore was on the plane.

He was thus unable to join us on our club tour of Nyasaland, southern Rhodesia and Ghana. When I called him into my office to break the news, I said with contrived severity: 'You won't be coming with us on tour.' Then, as his face fell, I added with a smile: '. . . because you're going to Chile with England.' Moore's face was now a mixture of surprise and pleasure, and even perhaps a flush of anger at my 'bad news, good news' way of letting him know. One thing is certain – my pleasure at Moore's selection was at least as great as his own.

Moore's selection was kept quiet for a day or two, to keep the pressure off him before they left, but Winterbottom then decided to take a chance and played him at right-half in the warm-up game against Peru. That one unexpected invitation was all Moore needed and he played in all the World Cup games in Chile. He had come to stay. A hundred or so more caps were on their way.

Jimmy Adamson, Burnley's captain, much respected and highly experienced, was Walter's right-hand man on the trip, and when he got back, he told me he had noticed one or two little faults in Moore's game. 'Bobby's a bad passer,' was one comment. He meant Moore's passing was erratic under pressure. 'Well, I wouldn't worry about that,' I replied. 'He'll cope because once he knows about a fault, he irons it out.'

I knew there were still a few good habits to be ingrained into Moore, but this was just a matter of time.

Moore's timing was impeccable in everything – even the start of his professional career coincided with the removal of the maximum wage, and this led to an early difference of opinion. I offered £28 and Moore wanted £30. This sounds ridiculous now, but in those days a couple of pounds mattered – a point emphasised by the fact that we both felt it was worth arguing about. I was brought up never to spend what I hadn't got; and as West Ham were not a rich club, my attitude to their money was exactly the same. The players used to think I was a Scrooge. I didn't like disagreements over money because they pinpointed one of every manager's main difficulties. One moment, in his office, he is expected to argue about money. The next moment, on the pitch, he is expected to ask for blood. But in the office or on the pitch, it was my job to do right by the club. And yes, Moore and the rest of the players eventually got their £30.

The only player with whom I would compare Moore is Franz Beckenbauer of West Germany. Beckenbauer had a bit more pace but the quickness of Moore's mind compensated for that. He read the game uncannily well, his anticipation always seemed to give him a head start, he was icily cold at moments of high stress and his positional sense was impeccable. He was at his best when his best was most needed and his concentration never let up. He made football look a simple and lovely art.

Hurst was barely holding his own as a First Division footballer when I joined West Ham. He had played eight league games in two seasons and, at best, he was promising to become a strong, honest wing-half with no claim on history. He was handsomely built, always willing and loved to go forward, but his game lacked foundation. He was useless at accepting responsibility. I told him early on: 'You're a horrible defender. When the ball's behind you, you don't even know where it is.'

I still felt Hurst had qualities we could work on, however, and I politely said no when Arthur Rowe, Crystal Palace's manager, suggested him in part-exchange for Johnny Byrne in March 1962 [Rowe was persuaded to take West Ham centre-forward Ron Brett instead]. Arthur knew Geoff's father, Charlie, from his playing days. Charlie, a useful player with Oldham and one or two other clubs, had moved south to link up with Arthur in his Southern League days at

Chelmsford. This was how Geoff, who was born in Ashton-Under-Lyne, came to live in east London. Charlie, I think, would have liked Geoff to play for his old boss at Selhurst. They felt Geoff wasn't making enough headway at West Ham.

I had attempted to open up a place at right-half for Hurst by letting Andy Malcolm, a hard and reliable club man, go to Chelsea in exchange for Ron Tindall, but Geoff did nothing to change my opinion that this wasn't his best position. A brief memory, though, kept coming back to me. In my Arsenal days, we had played West Ham in a friendly, after we'd both been knocked out of the FA Cup, and I could recall being impressed by a young chap who played up front. His name was Hurst.

That memory led to an idea, and soon after the start of the 1962–63 season, I asked Hurst to have a go in attack. He put up a half-argument but I made it clear to him that if he was going to have a future in the game, it wouldn't be at wing-half. I told him: 'I want someone who is strong and aggressive, and not afraid to work in attack, and I think you're the man. It's my judgement that's at risk, and I won't hold it against you if it doesn't work. All I want you to do is play your natural game. Do the things you want to do and like doing. That will do for now and, in time, we'll add the rest. Have a go . . .'

He did, too, and we beat Liverpool at Upton Park by a goal to nil. Geoff Hurst was on the right road.

Hurst had a lot to learn, but he was a coach's dream. Nobody could have worked harder. He listened and practised and kept on practising, and the improvement in his game was remarkable. He learnt to take the ball coming from behind, and worked on his heading and shooting from all distances and angles. His control improved 100 per cent, his mobility acquired a new edge and he quickly grasped the principles of making and using space.

'You can make the stupidest of runs in the First Division, but defenders still won't dare let you go,' I told him at the start. 'Look at it like that, and you'll drag your opponents all over the place. Even when you're going nowhere or heading in the wrong direction, you will always make space for others.' He then began to realise that once he made room for others, that room was there for him as well. He would drag his opponents out and then come back in himself. His strength was his legs; his endless running and direction-changing were phenomenal. He was also as brave as they come.

Hurst was our leading goalscorer that season, but it was in America the following summer [when Lyall was in charge of the squad] that he proved to everyone – including himself – that he had completed the transition from midfield to attack. He scored nine goals in ten games.

A partnership that was very special developed between Hurst and Byrne. To begin with, Hurst just took the weight off Byrne. Their worth to each other was a bit hit and miss. Byrne was the star, once he found his real form, and Hurst the straight man. But gradually, a real relationship grew.

They were opposites in appearance and style. Hurst was the strong type, Budgie the dapper twinkler. But it was this contrast that made them so effective.

Between them, they had everything to undermine opposing defences. Hurst, with his late angled runs, his controlled power and aggression, his persistence and selflessness, posed one sort of problem, while Byrne, with his deft touches, instant control, ability to beat his man, quickness over the first vital yards and cheekiness presented another. Both, too, knew exactly where the net was. They got more than 40 goals between them in each of their first two full seasons together.

Byrne helped make Hurst, but in the end they were as complementary as bacon and eggs.

Jimmy Hill once put together a 15-minute montage for television of Hurst running off the ball and I think this should have been shown to every club in the country. His movement was fantastic. I wonder if the fans on the terraces at these games always recognised what he was doing.

A Bolton director once said to me after West Ham had knocked seven past them in a League Cup tie: 'Hurst reminds me of Nat Lofthouse.'

'Afraid not,' I replied. 'Nat did his work at the far post. This fellow Hurst gets to the ball anywhere. Far post, yes, but also near the ground and at the near post. It's a different game.'

Hurst's ability at the near post was something which developed over a period. Not only for Hurst either; it was something which involved everybody. The vulnerability of defences to a strike or knock-on in this area had come home to me again during the 1966 World Cup finals, when I was a member of FIFA's technical study group. During the game between Hungary and Brazil at Goodison Park [in which Brazil suffered their first defeat in the competition for 12 years] Ferenc Bene scored a near-post goal from a cross by Florian Albert. It only happened once in this game, but it struck me that in English football such a goal was scored by accident rather than design. Here was a chance for profit.

Back at West Ham, we put down a couple of cones, one on each side of the field. Each player had to take the ball up to one of the cones, screw the ball around it, as if it was a man, and then cross to the near post area – between the post and the edge of the six-yard box. Johnny Sissons and Harry Redknapp got it to perfection. At the near post, we had Geoff Hurst, Martin Peters and other front men hitting [heading or striking] the ball as it came to them. They knew roughly where the ball was going to drop, the rest was up to them. This practice tested technique; it improved technique and it paid off handsomely.

The near-post threat proved difficult to counter even when it was expected. We played Manchester City, for example, and Malcolm Allison spelt out the dangers to his defence which included a new full-back he had just signed from Hearts, Arthur Mann. But Hurst and Peters each scored a goal at Mann's near post and Malcolm said to me afterwards: 'It's no good talking to them is it? Not with your two!'

A lot of sides attack at the near post now. Some get it right, some never will. But back in the 1960s, it was new. The near post was the soft underbelly of many defences and many people in the game did not understand what was happening. Peters would ghost up from midfield, timing his run to perfection, while Hurst would confuse the defence by going to the far post and then switching suddenly at the last moment to the near. Newcastle's John McNamee was once taken to the far post by Hurst, and was still there as Hurst knocked the ball in at the near post! People used to say we were lucky. Week after week.

I cherish our association. Geoff Hurst was a loyal club man, a brilliant team man and a great player himself. Can any manager ask for more?

Peters was the most gifted of them all. He had so much talent that it would be ridiculous to claim that anybody 'discovered' him. He was an outstanding player as a boy; he was always at the front of the shop window as a youth. Every club with half an eye open wanted him, including Chelsea, Arsenal, Spurs and Fulham. But he was cockney, a real east Londoner, and Wally St Pier [West Ham's chief scout] talked the same language. There was never much doubt that Peters would join West Ham.

Peters was a natural games-player and he looked the part. He was tall, lithe and well balanced, and he had a nice easy relationship with the ball which made him look as if he was never in a hurry. He did everything so perfectly, he made it look too easy. But even with all those advantages, he had his early problems; his versatility told against him.

I gave Peters his first league game at Easter 1962. The side had been playing reasonably well, but that is rarely good enough, and I felt the time was ripe for a gee-up. It was also the right time of the season for an experiment or two. So I dropped five players, including Phil Woosnam and Geoff Hurst, and Peters took Hurst's place at right-half. We beat Cardiff at Upton Park and I decided to play the same team against Arsenal, also at home, the following day.

Early in the second half, Lawrie Leslie [West Ham's keeper]

broke a finger diving at the feet of an Arsenal forward, so John Lyall went in goal and Peters was switched to left-back. We drew 3–3 after being 3–1 behind. As Peters had done well at left-back, I kept him there for the return with Cardiff at Ninian Park on the Easter Monday. More drama was to come. Brian Rhodes, Leslie's deputy, dislocated his collar bone after about an hour and Peters went into goal. He had proved himself a useful keeper in practice and in one reserve game he actually started in goal. He was a player who could turn his hand to anything.

But the question remained: what was his best position?

Peters played regularly the following season, mostly at wing-half but always ready to fill in where required. He was the answer to a manager's prayer, although the fans did not always appreciate him. He brought refinement to whatever job he did, and I think some people mistook that for softness. He was not a typical English player and the terraces did not relate to him. In a way his ability went above their heads.

I had no reservations about him, however, and in that same 1962–63 season, I happily recommended Peters to Walter Winterbottom for an England Under-23 cap. Walter rang me to say one or two players had pulled out of his side to play Belgium at Plymouth. He wanted Bobby Moore to play at left-half. I said: 'You don't want Bobby, he's a full international now. Have the other one, Martin Peters. He's ready.' So Peters played, scored twice in a 6–1 win and was England's best player.

The first hiccup in Peters' career came halfway through our FA Cup season in 1963–64. It followed an 8–2 thumping by Blackburn at Upton Park on Boxing Day. It was a terrible game, technically, but Blackburn capitalised on our mistakes, getting the ball inside our full-backs and into space which Fred Pickering and John Byrom made good use of. We had our chances – the score should have been about 8–6 – but didn't take them.

I deliberately did not go into the dressing-room afterwards. I went upstairs to my office, just in case I was going to have a heart attack! I wanted to avoid saying anything I might regret, and also to have a few moments' thought in peace. The return game at Blackburn was only 48 hours later, so time was precious. After a while, I wrote down a team for Ewood Park. There were nine changes. Then I wrote another, and this time there were eight changes. Then another . . . seven changes. And another . . . six. The process continued until I felt I got the team exactly right; and now there was just one change! Eddie Bovington for Martin Peters at right-half.

Peters was going through a lean patch by his own standards and a knee injury was also bothering him. His style meant that if his movement or confidence was affected, his whole game suffered; he could not compensate by pure physical effort. It was not in his nature. Bovington, on the other hand, was a gritty, efficient player, who would give us firm control in midfield and who was itching for a chance to prove himself.

The change paid off. We were able to pull in our full-backs and force the ball wide. Bryan Douglas, Blackburn's England winger, who was a real trick-man with the ball and who had never been pinned down at Upton Park, was no longer a threat. We won 3–1, and that same side went right on, unchanged, to win the FA Cup.

Peters came in for only the odd game, to fill a gap created by injury, and like any player with pride, he was far from happy. He eventually came to see me just before the Cup final, obviously nervous and worried, and told me I had cost him his life's ambition – to play at Wembley. I said: 'The side is settled and playing well. But I bet you one thing – you will play more times at Wembley than I eat in the restaurant there.' I went on: 'Everything's gone right for you in your career so far. There have been no problems. You have a dodgy knee and things aren't going well. This is a test of character for you. This is where you stand up or fall down. You've got to fight your way in again.'

I knew his time would come but it wasn't then, not as part of our Cup team.

Martin then said he was fed up with being a 'general

dogsbody'. He said: 'What is my best position? It's all right being a utility player, but I never know where I am going to play. You're making use of me.'

That was a question I could not answer immediately. I promised him that we would work something out, and the solution, which came the following season, was simply to give him a free hand. Broadly, he filled the gap behind our strikers, playing wide when he chose to, pushing forward when he wanted to – a role without restriction.

It was a job which only a player of Peters' quality could have done. He really was the complete all-rounder. He had a steely temperament, intelligence, ideas, subtlety and vision. His long legs covered the ground surprisingly quickly, he volleyed beautifully, he was an artist in the air, he tackled surprisingly strongly and he moved the ball to order. He always seemed to have a pay-off pass ready, often knocking it away first time where others would have needed a second touch, and all through his game ran an uncanny sense of timing.

He knew when to move and where to move and, importantly, he never gave up. Sometimes, he would make a 20-yard run and there would be nothing at the end of it. But he would go again and again and again – and that is hard work. His understanding of space, and his timing, were delightful.

I don't want to sound boastful, but I think Peters is perhaps a player that only West Ham could have produced. I believe he would have done well with half a dozen other clubs, but it was our style and philosophy which enabled him to flower properly. He did not need to adjust with us, because he found the understanding he needed at Upton Park. He had players around him who were on the same wavelength. We were right for him. He was right for us. The result was a player who did full justice to all his talents.

To Greenwood, having three stars of this calibre was like 'hitting the jackpot on the pools three weeks in a row'. However, while stating that they gave West Ham the best years of their careers, and brought him 'great pride and satisfaction', they also caused 'thumping headaches'. Strange as it might seem, this particularly applied to Moore. Greenwood wrote:

> All three [Moore, Peters and Hurst] changed as men [after steering England to their 1966 World Cup triumph]. They became more assured and more ambitious, and all of them, at different times and in their own way, asked to leave West Ham. They felt the grass – any grass – would be greener on the other side. Each got his way eventually but in West Ham's time. Peters went to Tottenham [1970], Hurst to Stoke [1972] and Moore to Fulham [1974]. But before then, I could have sold them many times. They were the hottest properties in football.
>
> I even wanted to sack Moore at one point, and our relationship became unhappy and strained. There was an icy corridor between us.
>
> Moore, in fact, refused to sign a contract in the months before the World Cup. He wanted richer pastures and I know Spurs would have liked him. We had no intention of letting Moore go, either before or after the World Cup. It was deadlock; problems loomed. Football Association officials were concerned that unless Moore signed and became a properly registered player, he would not even be allowed to play in the World Cup. Just imagine the rumpus that would have caused. Alf Ramsey was keen that he should sign because he did not want a captain with other things on his mind.
>
> Eventually, I was called to the England headquarters, and this time there were no hiccups. I had a chat with Alf, and then with Bobby. The signature was a formality.
>
> By this time, I had taken the club captaincy away from Moore. His attitude clearly meant that he was less than 100 per cent for the club, and I gave the job to Johnny Byrne, who bubbled with enthusiasm. It was not a difficult decision because

it made the point that no player was bigger than his club. Moore did not show a flicker of emotion when I told him: I am not sure he ever did show any. Only once in all my years with him did he congratulate a player for scoring a goal. That was when Ted MacDougall scored his first goal for West Ham after joining us from Manchester United and Moore ran half the length of the field to him. Normally, he regarded such a gesture as a waste of energy.

Phil Woosnam, my first West Ham captain, was always popping into the office, full of ideas and chat but Moore never followed this line. He took responsibility but led by example more than anything else. Moore had presence and style, and above all he had standards. That was his real strength. He always put in a good performance on the field no matter what battles he was fighting. In action, he was always a first-class professional. He had pride.

It has been said of Moore that he was a big-occasion player who did not put himself out in lesser combat. Not true. He was a big-occasion player – but only in the sense that he somehow scaled new heights when it was necessary for him to do so.

Moore also had nerves of steel, as he showed during the Bogotá incident just before the 1970 World Cup when he was ludicrously accused of stealing a bracelet. I cannot imagine many players of this or any other generation who would come sailing through that kind of experience and become one of the outstanding players of a World Cup tournament. Nobody could have handled it better; and great credit to him.

Off the field, however, we had a problem. I felt he became very aloof, locked in a world of his own, and although his cold detachment was a strength on the field, and even a shield in situations like the one in Bogotá, it was an attitude which made things very difficult in the small, everyday world of a football club. Moore even started to give the impression that he was ignoring me at team-talks. He would glance around with a blasé look on his face, eyes glazed, in a way that suggested he had nothing to learn. 'Who needs a manager?' he seemed to be saying. The danger was that other, less experienced players would believe what they saw.

I called him into my office and told him: 'Don't give the impression you're not listening. You may be kidding some of the players but it doesn't wash with me. Whenever I ask for something to be done on the field, you're the first to do it. I know you're listening to every word. So why the act?'

He did not argue.

It was impossible to get close to Moore. There was a big corner of himself that he would not or could not give. To begin with, I think it was a sort of protective act, but eventually the act became reality. He seemed to step inside an image from which he couldn't escape.

It worried me because I knew what a nice person he was at heart. I remembered him as a lad, full of enthusiasm and determination, and the way we had shared our passion for the game. I had given him his first chance with the England Youth and Under-23 teams and recommended him for his first full cap. I had shaped his understanding of the game and his attitude to it, and moved him into the specialised defensive position he made his own. I had tremendous faith in Moore and would never listen to criticism of him. Lucy [Greenwood's wife] says that even at home, I would never hear a word against him. It hurt that he could be so cold to someone who cared about him and who had helped him so much.

I suppose it was a case of different personalities not gelling, and this was my fault as much as his. I tried to bridge the gap between us once or twice, but it never worked. The lowest point of all was the Blackpool affair in January 1971 [when Moore, together with team-mates Brian Dear, Clyde Best, Jimmy Greaves, and the club physiotherapist, Rob Jenkins, were drinking in a nightclub on the eve of a 4–0 FA Cup defeat at Blackpool]. It led to my asking the West Ham directors to sack them. I felt so let down. I had the five in and, one by one, they apologised but insisted they had done nothing wrong. They had just 'gone for a drink', nothing more, nothing less.

Moore even said he thought I'd let him down by not denying the story to the press. Moore and the other four let everyone down. I felt this, so did the fans and so, in a way, did the newspapers. If there was no harm in a spot of night-life before a game they would not have given the story the treatment they did. But the issue went deeper than this. There was a heavy social scene available to many of the players. We had been successful, one or two players uniquely so, and inevitably there were queues of people wanting to latch on. Invitations rolled in.

Moore's world was particularly big. He would travel with us on an away trip in casual clothes but before we got back to London he would disappear into the toilet for a while and then emerge all dressed up in immaculate fashion. His wife, Tina, would be waiting for him and at ten o'clock on a Saturday night, they would go into town. There was nothing wrong with this. But the gap between what is acceptable and what a player thinks is acceptable is growing all the time. There is a right time for a drink and a wrong time. A nightclub in Blackpool a few hours before an important cup tie is the wrong time.

Moore the player would have improved any team in the world. Brian Clough even decided that he would be an asset to his Championship side at Derby and made an attempt to buy him [at the start of the 1973–74 season]. Moore got uptight [about West Ham's unwillingness to part with him] and accused me of standing in his way. What I did not know at the time was that Clough had been in touch with Moore privately, but the word always gets back sooner or later. Football is like a village community. Nothing is secret for very long.

In all his years with us, a side without Moore seemed inconceivable. Even in his last year with us, I would get threats of bomb damage to my house if I dared let him go. I received them by phone and by letter and, far from worrying me, I used to think: 'Good, it shows people care.' Moore *was* West Ham. But not even a man like him lasts forever and eventually Mick McGivern, who we'd bought from Newcastle, started to do a good job at the back whenever Bobby was injured or out of touch. I felt the time had come when we could let him go. We had talked of a free transfer, but in the end I worked things out differently. We sold him to Fulham for £50,000 for West Ham and £25,000 for Moore. Not a bad handshake.

Geoff Hurst was a man I would have been happy to have at West Ham forever. I was delighted later on to make him an England coach [when Greenwood was England manager]. His three goals at Wembley in 1966 did more than win the World Cup for England. They reshaped his whole career and personality. He had always been a nice chap with a bit of style, but after that historic hat-trick he grew in stature as both a player and a person. But he never became selfish. He was always willing to help others.

Hurst would have liked a chance to play for one of the country's biggest clubs but he never made an issue of it. Matt Busby wanted him to join Manchester United [in the 1967–68 season]. Hurst was very interested because he seemed to have achieved almost everything he could with us and the call of Old Trafford was a powerful one. It offered him a new challenge and a new world and, in fact, Manchester United rounded off that season by winning the European Cup. But Geoff took my refusal well. He always did.

Later on, however, I promised Hurst that if a good offer came along, which would give him a chance to make some money, I would not stand in his way. Stoke eventually said all the right things in 1972 and, although Geoff was still playing well and the fee was modest [£80,000] I thought the timing was correct. Geoff did well out of the move, and that was the main thing.

It was a personal opinion which finally ended Peters' career with West Ham. He became convinced that the other two, Moore and Hurst, were getting most of the credit and the rewards after 1966. He saw himself as a sort of quiz question – 'Who scored England's other goal in the World Cup final?' – with most people getting the answer wrong. Martin was a very likeable person, but he became fed up and eventually sure in his own mind that things would be different elsewhere.

Tottenham's Bill Nicholson, signed Peters in 1970 in a then British record £200,000 deal which involved the departure of Jimmy Greaves to West Ham in exchange. Tottenham unquestionably got the better of the deal, with Peters making almost 300 first-team appearances in his five years there, and collecting two League Cup-winners' medals and a UEFA Cup-winners' medal. He then made a similar number of appearances for Norwich before the curtain was pulled down on his career, as Sheffield United player-manager.

The highlight of Moore's career after West Ham was when he and Alan Mullery steered Second Division Fulham to the 1975 FA Cup final – ironically against the Hammers, who went on to win 2–0 through two Alan Taylor goals. Moore also played in the North American League before trying his hand at management with Oxford City and then Southend.

Hurst made more than 100 appearances for Stoke before ending his league playing career with a brief spell at West Bromwich Albion. After a season with Seattle Sounders in the United States, he was appointed player-manager of Telford United and then became manager of Chelsea. In addition to being the only member of the trio to have been a First Division manager, Hurst added another string to his bow on this side of the game by helping Ron Greenwood with the running of the England team.

Nowadays, Hurst and Peters are prominent figures in a major insurance company; and, as one would expect of two men who played such a big part in the greatest moment in England's soccer history, both are still much in demand for personal appearances.

Sadly, of course, Moore is no longer with us. When he died on

Wednesday, 24 February 1993, two months short of his 52nd birthday, Upton Park was turned into a shrine. The Hammers had lost their favourite son; and for Peters and Hurst – not to mention Ron Greenwood, the trio's football godfather – the sense of mourning was inevitably particularly acute.

West Ham's first home match following Moore's death was against Wolves, and was marked by fans coming on to the pitch to lay flowers on the centre spot. Even more poignant, though, was the sight of Peters, Hurst and Greenwood following them with a giant wreath designed in the form of Moore's old West Ham number 6 shirt.

Today, the memory of Moore lives on at Upton Park through the fact that the club's south stand is named after him. It is a constant reminder to West Ham diehards of what their team was like when the imperious Moore, a blue-blood of world football if ever there was one, was out there on the field along with Peters and Hurst.

CHAPTER 2

Bobby Moore, Martin Peters and Geoff Hurst

It takes a number of different ingredients to make a great football team. But if you adhere to the view that the building of one should start at the back, Bobby Moore represents a stunning first brick by any standards.

Moore's defensive qualities alone would have made him the perfect starting point for the West Ham dream team. But it was the manner in which he went about his job, the part he played in shaping the approach of the men in front of him, that puts him head and shoulders above anyone else who might be considered for the crucial role of back line general.

So easy did Moore make his job look that he might just as well have taken the field with a cigar in one hand and a glass of brandy in the other. There was a regal air about his performances, which always led you to believe that he was playing well within himself. No matter who he was playing against, or how much pressure he was under, Moore did his job – usually perfectly – with the minimum fuss and bother. It was beneath his dignity to resort to the physical tactics deployed by many other British defenders. Moore put it this way: 'I look on tackling as a skill. Any time I see a defender just whacking through the back of a forward's legs to get at a ball, that to me is ignorance. You can't win the ball if you've got a body in front of you. You don't have to go kicking people up in the air to be a good tackler.'

'I have thought about the whole business of petty fouling and retaliation. There are players who make a point of trying to annoy you from the kick-off, either by physical or verbal niggles. An angry player is less effective and there is something to be gained in pushing a bloke until he loses his temper. I have my own way of annoying that kind of opposition. I pretend they don't exist.'

Quite apart from the adverse psychological effect this must have had on his opponents, just think of how his team-mates will have benefitted from having such a commanding, high-class figure behind them.

Ken Brown, the big, amiable centre-half who played alongside Moore for much of his West Ham career – from 1952 to 1967 – recalls: 'He was fabulous, you couldn't get anyone better than him. I was a natural defender, and when the ball was knocked into our box, the first thing in my mind was to get it away first time. It was more by luck than judgement if it fell to one of our players – I just wanted the ball out of our box and, as far as I was concerned, if I stopped the centre-forward scoring, I had done my job. But Mooro would want to bring it down on his chest, on his knee – you know, he wanted to play football and to him, just hoofing the ball up the park was taking the easy way out. Whenever the ball was knocked into his area, I always took up a covering position behind him just in case he missed or lost it. I thought: "He's going to come a cropper one day." But in all the matches I played with him, I can't ever recall that happening.

'He was so much in control of situations. His anticipation was brilliant.

'I remember having a bit of barney with Ron [Greenwood] over this. When the other team had a corner, I thought we should all be defending flat-out, making sure we were behind the ball, all that sort of thing. Our keeper would come and get it and then who would be the first person calling for it outside the box? It would be Bobby. I said: "What the bloody hell is he doing out there when he should be in the box with us?" What I did not appreciate then was that Bobby knew as soon as the corner was taken that the keeper was going to get the ball – he was a step ahead of most other people. Again, I can't ever recall his messing things up.

'He was uncanny. Eddie Bailey [the England international inside-forward then playing for Tottenham] once said that the best way of dealing with Bobby was to have a man marking him. I thought: "What's he on about, silly sod? How can you mark a defender?" It was unheard of. But in hindsight, I think he was probably right. Bobby, with his control and vision, was so good at starting attacking moves that any team who could stop him could go a long way towards stopping West Ham.'

Easier said than done – even in West Ham's matches against the top teams. Indeed, the bigger the match, the more that Moore appeared to stamp his authority on it.

Take his Wembley appearances, for example, and especially the European Cup-Winners' Cup final against TSV Munich 1860 in 1965, when he led the Hammers to a 2–0 victory that still ranks as the greatest achievement in the club's history.

Playing at Wembley can do strange things to a professional footballer – even experienced players have been known to 'freeze' on this stage. But for Moore, then in the early stages of a glittering England career that was to bring him 108 England caps, Wembley was like his relaxing country home.

As far as big club matches were concerned, Moore had worn West Ham's shirt at Wembley for the first time the previous year, when leading the Hammers to their 3–2 win over Preston in the FA Cup final. Despite the number of goals and the exciting scoring pattern (West Ham were twice behind), the Hammers' performance was not as polished as they would have wished. That they made such heavy weather of getting the better of a Second Division team was perhaps understandable. This, after all, had been the club's first FA Cup final appearance since the famous 'white horse' final of 1923; their team, with an average age of just 24, was one of the youngest to reach the final since the war; and much of their adrenalin had been used up already in a surprise 3–1 semi-final victory over Manchester United at Hillsborough.

Many regular Moore-watchers had rated his display against

United – in driving rain and ankle-deep mud – as the most majestic of his career. Moore was the defensive rock on which the flair of United attacking stars like Denis Law and Bobby Charlton foundered. But the most abiding memory of him in that epic battle came 11 minutes from the end, with the Hammers striving to hang on to a 2–1 lead and United appearing to have them on the ropes.

Moore beat Pat Crerand to a loose ball near the touchline, just inside the West Ham half, and at that point no West Ham supporter would have complained had he booted it as far up the field as he could to give his tired team some breathing space. But that, of course, was not Moore's style. Instead, he took the ball past Crerand, down the line, and ran 30 yards with it towards the United corner flag. Most professionals in that position would have been content to just take the ball into the circle and indulge in the time-wasting exercise of keeping it there. Moore, though, spotted Geoff Hurst in a position to put United two-down, and produced the perfect pass to invite Hurst to scamper through and drive the ball into the net.

As a test of technique and temperament, though, the Hammers' clash with TSV Munich 1860 was set at an even higher level.

West Ham's ability to compete with the best at European level had been underlined two years earlier when they reached the final of an international close-season tournament in the United States and were unlucky to lose to Czechoslovakia's Dukla Prague. Despite the result, Ron Greenwood, never the easiest of men to please when it came to assessing the quality of his team's football, described the performance as 'the most technically perfect display I have ever seen from a team I have been connected with'. Dukla's outstanding Josef Masopust was equally impressed: 'West Ham will be a top grade side in two years.'

Those who tuned into the European Cup-Winners' Cup final, the 100,000 Wembley crowd and the then biggest-ever TV audience for a midweek match in Britain, had good cause to remember those words as the Hammers and their German rivals produced a contest which was packed with superb attacking play from both sides and which was like a dream come true for any connoisseur of the finer points of the game.

It was certainly a dream come true for Alan Sealy, a speedy right-winger who had come into the side in place of Peter Brabrook and who scored both goals in a 2–0 Hammers victory. Sealy was not as clever on the ball as Brabrook, but as he was to emphasise against Munich, he was more direct and got through more work off the ball. Brian Dear might also have been pinching himself, given that he had started the season as West Ham's A-team centre-forward and would not have been in their Wembley line-up had Johnny Byrne not been unavailable because of injury.

But most of all, it was a dream come true for Greenwood, whose tactical master plan involving Dear operating as the Hammers' only central striker and Geoff Hurst in a central midfield role paid off more handsomely than anyone can have envisaged. Greenwood preferred to dwell afterwards not on the result (which would have been even more impressive but for the acrobatics of Munich's Yugoslavian international keeper, Radenkovic, and John Sissons' ill-fortune in twice firing against the post), but the manner in which it was achieved.

'I said to my players before the start: "Here's the chance to show the world what we can do," and that is exactly what they did. Three years of hard work and faith went into our win. Our principles were justified. We proved that football at its best was a game of beauty and intelligence. Players and ball were in happy harmony, while skill and method flourished together. Ideas and passes flowed. For me, it was fulfilment.'

As professional footballers are generally a straightforward, uncomplicated species, this lyrical description of West Ham's play will probably have been lost on most of Greenwood's pupils; however, one who did not need a part-time tutor to get on the same wavelength was Robert Moore. Significantly, while Greenwood was talking about the 'technical perfection' in West Ham's performance, he could not resist the temptation to mention Moore as an example. 'This was Bobby Moore's greatest game for West Ham,' he said.

Though it might seem churlish to single out any individuals in what was a stupendous team performance by the Hammers that night, it is tempting to suggest that something Moore did after only two minutes – when he hit a superb 40-yard pass to Hurst on the left, which led to the first scoring chance – was, in its way, just as imporant as the two second-half strikes with which Sealy brought them their victory. For West Ham, the tone of their approach to the game had been set. Three minutes later, Moore played Dear through for a shot which hit the Munich net, but was ruled offside. This is how the West Ham fanzine, *Fortune's Always Hiding*, described Moore's involvement in the battle between the two teams to establish an early ascendancy:

> Munich began to get more into the game [after Hurst and Sissons had also gone close to giving West Ham the lead] but Moore twice intercepted with immaculate timing. With the West Ham captain now in command, carrying the ball forward and passing accurately with both feet, West Ham swept forward as the first choruses of 'Bubbles' swept around the stadium.
>
> The first half ended as it had begun, with West Ham's flowing football causing the German rearguard tremendous problems. Hurst, who began his football career in midfield, showed what a great footballer he was by winning the ball and passing it intelligently, slowing the game down then quickly stepping up the tempo. Boyce and Peters worked equally hard in midfield, whilst up front, the pace of Sealy on the right and the constant interchanging of Dear and Sissons often left the Munich defence bewildered.
>
> If West Ham were good in the first half, they were simply magnificent in the second. Moore began to move upfield more frequently and the whole team played with inspired self-belief.

The first tangible reward came after 70 minutes, when Boyce made an interception in midfield, carried the ball forward deep into the Munich half and slipped the ball past two defenders to

Sealy, who hit a right-foot shot into the roof of the net. Sealy celebrated with a somersault; and just a couple of minutes later that sense of elation engulfed him again when the ball from a Moore free-kick broke off Peters, and he swooped to prod it home from close range.

For the super-cool Moore, a man who rarely showed his emotions, it seemed tantamount to being just another good day at the office. As it turned out, it was also excellent practice for what was to follow for Moore – and England – at Wembley the following year. As Moore held the European Cup-Winners' Cup aloft, the BBC's match commentator, Kenneth Wolstenholme, remarked: 'Who knows, in just over a year's time he might be standing on the same spot with the World Cup in his hands.'

*   *   *

Martin Peters has always been famous for Sir Alf Ramsey's description of him as a player who was 'ten years ahead of his time'.

The compliment stemmed from Ramsey's vision of teams of the future packed with players capable of interchanging positions, as opposed to sticking rigidly to one specific job or role – the sort of players for which Ajax were to become renowned when their 'total football' swept them to three successive European Cup triumphs at the start of the 1970s. Ramsey was not alone in eulogising over Peters' advanced soccer intellect. Ron Greenwood was another, of course – and so, too, was Bobby Moore.

As Greenwood has pointed out, Peters was the most gifted of West Ham's famous 1966 World Cup trio and in Moore's biography, *Bobby Moore, the Life and Times of a Sporting Hero*, by Jeff Powell, the Hammers' captain suggested that Peters' presence was one of the main reasons why the club was able to win the European Cup-Winners' Cup.

'It still surprises a lot of people to be told that Martin Peters was not in our 1964 FA Cup final team. Martin is remembered as being as much part of West Ham as Geoff [Hurst] and myself.

But Eddie Bovington was the wing-half in 1964 and Martin didn't get the position until we went into Europe. That worked out well in its way. But in the Cup-Winners' Cup, you needed more skill and Martin added an extra quality to our game. In addition to all his talent, he had vision and awareness and a perfect sense of timing.'

That sense of timing, which was brought into sharp focus by the late runs which enabled him to 'ghost' into scoring positions on the blind side of opponents, brought him 100 goals in 364 West Ham matches, and 20 in 67 games for England – a superb record for a midfield player. However, it is on the cards that Moore will have struck a discordant note with Peters when, in selecting the best England XI from all the men he had played with or against, he named his old colleague as the substitute on the basis of Peters' versatility.

'Such talent,' Moore said of him. 'He was obviously known as a midfield player who scored goals. Yet he could be a tremendous centre-half because of great ability in the air and long legs for tackling. Not the quickest man on earth, but he would never leave himself in a position where he could be vulnerable. Martin was a natural sportsman from the start, good at any game he tried. We might be travelling somewhere and see people playing an unusual game and Martin would ask to try it and be good at it right away.'

That Peters is likely to have viewed all this with mixed feelings soon becomes apparent when you read the part of his autobiography (aptly titled *Goals from Nowhere*) relating to his public image. Peters admitted that when Ramsey made that comment about his being ten years ahead of his time, during the 1967–68 season, he was up half the night thinking – and fretting – about it.

He said: 'It looked, at first, to be the sort of thing someone says about you before they show you the door, the sort of consolation compliment a budding author might get on a rejection slip. But the longer I thought about it, the more I saw that not only was it a compliment, coming from where it did, but that it gave me an identity. Heaven knows how badly I needed one.

'Up until then, despite reaching the halfway stage of a successful and rewarding career, I had been haunted by the feeling that somehow I didn't fit; that I was some sort of phantom footballer playing a vital role in games of the highest level yet remaining comparatively unrecognised and unknown.

'I felt that an awful lot of people who watched me play for West Ham and England did not have the faintest idea what I was supposed to be doing out there. And because they were vague about my position they were vague about me and about whether I was really necessary.

'Whenever people put forward their suggestion for an England team I never seemed to be in it. A small point maybe, but I remember my wife Cathy looking up from the paper one night and saying: "The only person who ever picks you for England is Alf Ramsey!"

'Almost every well-known or fairly well-known footballer has an instant identity, a definite part to play, a part that helps mould his public image. Think of Bobby Moore, and you see the cool, unflappable defensive general. Think of Geoff Hurst, and the word "goalscorer" flashes through the mind. Think of Martin Peters . . . and you'll probably have to think twice. At least that is the way I felt.

'It is fairly obvious that I am a midfield player. I go forward looking for goals. I go back to help the defence. I tackle. I mark. I have specific jobs and yet I am a free agent. I try to be wherever there is space and where I am needed. It is all very simple, really. It is also very vague.

'I do just about everything and if that sounds immodest I can't help it. And as a player of many parts instead of just one, I seem to melt into the background of a game as far as the spectator is concerned. I was getting resigned to this sort of existence until Sir Alf came out with the words that I was ten years ahead of my time. Here at last was an explanation. I hadn't even been invented.'

Peters expressed the hope that, when the day came when a football team comprised a goalkeeper and ten 'complete' players, the players of that day 'will not feel so wretched about being versatile as I have'.

He continued: 'In December 1966 I played number 7 for West Ham at Burnley. It meant that at the age of just 23, I had played every position on the field, including goalkeeper, in Football League games for West Ham. A couple of days later, the *Daily Express* ran a picture of me pointing to a team arranged in the usual group. The only thing unusual about the picture was that my head was on every body. They called it "The One-Man Team". I was proud of that picture, proud of the versatility that had enabled me to play in every position. Yet I had the same old feeling that people were not impressed.

'There is one word in football that I detest and used to fear. It has been frequently applied to me and I am still inclined to get annoyed with anyone who labels me with it. The word is "utility". My dictionary defines it as: "Usefulness, serviceableness, that which is useful". For a footballer to be called useful is to me almost as bad as being called useless. Do you know where the term "utility man" comes from? It is an old theatrical term which, my dictionary explains, means: "An actor employed to play unimportant parts, when required".'

But as far as the dictionary of football is concerned, the one word that everybody recognises and understands is 'goalscorer'. In that respect, if anything was to prove a turning point for Peters in terms of the public's perception of his value, it was his scoring record. Upon being switched to a free role just behind the orthodox strikers, Peters scored 17 in 60 matches for the Hammers in the 1965–66 season, 16 in 49 in 1966–67, 18 in 46 in 1967–68 and then a career-best total of 24 in 48 in 1968–69. As he said: 'I think I helped my own case [in 1968–69]. People notice goalscorers. In fact, I picked up a soccer magazine [at the end of the season] and nearly brought Horchchurch High Street to a halt. The magazine had held a poll for the best player in England – I was voted sixth. Those goals must have succeeded where my style of play failed.'

A number of those goals seemed ridiculously simple and straightforward – and to those with no appreciation of football as a thinking man's game, merely the end product of someone 'happening' to be in the right place at the right time. Yet one strike that will have done much to enhance Peters' image was West Ham's sixth goal in the astonishing 7–0 annihilation of Leeds in November 1966, when he dribbled past two Leeds defenders and hit a right-foot shot which went past the Leeds keeper, David Harvey, like an Exocet missile.

Peters himself is especially proud of a goal he scored against Gordon Banks, his goalkeeping colleague in England's 1966 World Cup-winning team, when Banks was playing for Stoke. 'Even if I say it myself, it was a fantastic goal.' One factor which made it such was Peters' part in the build-up to it. The move began with Peters getting his head to a long clearance by Banks, and directing the ball to Johnny Sissons. In a bewildering exchange of passes, the ball – as if on a pinball machine – was then moved from Sissons to Peters, from Peters to Dear, from Dear back to Peters and then from Peters to Sissons. Peters was then brought into the picture again and, taking the ball on the volley, he hit it into the net from 20 yards. Not even Banks, who had thwarted so many of the world's top strikers and who produced one of the greatest saves of all time when denying Pele a headed goal in the 1970 World Cup finals in Mexico, can ever have had to cope with a finish more powerful and accurate than that one from Peters. 'Gordon just stood there and gave me one of his Fernandel faces,' Peters says. 'It is probably as well I didn't hear what he said.'

In the modern game, Peters would have been the ideal player to fill the 'hole' between the midfielders and strikers, as Eric Cantona did for Manchester United. In view of his telepathic understanding with Hurst, the latter would surely have no compunction about playing up front on his own – an ever-increasing occurrence among today's top strikers – if he had someone like Peters to support him. There is a lot to be said for teams operating with only one recognised central striker, not the least of these being that the player has the full width of the field in which to manoeuvre and there is greater scope for team-mates in deeper areas to make runs into scoring positions. Ironically, of all the roles Peters had, the one as an orthodox centre-forward proved the least successful and enjoyable for him. 'But just by extending my range of activities into the penalty area whenever there was a chance, scoring has become an accepted part of my game,' he said. 'It is obvious that with strikers continually getting bogged down in deep defences, a lot can be gained by having players running from behind into scoring positions.'

One of the outstanding examples of this from Peters came in a West Ham match against Liverpool, when he scored with the 'hardest header' of his career. 'I started running, in anticipation of a chance, from just inside our own half,' he recalled. 'I was going like an express train when the cross came over and I met it square with my forehead. It flew in like a cannonball.'

In many ways, the relationship between Peters and Hurst was similar to the one that Manchester United's Teddy Sheringham and Newcastle's Alan Shearer have established in the England team in recent seasons. Peters was the equivalent of Sheringham, especially when it came to involving himself in the build-up play and creating chances for others.

That understanding between Hurst and Peters was highlighted many times for West Ham; and it certainly stood England in good stead in the 1966 World Cup – notably in the tough, bruising quarter-final against Argentina. When Argentina's captain, Antonio Rattin, was sent off with the score at 0–0 it seemed the break England needed to seize the initiative. However, what had been an exceptionally tight game became even tighter. The Argentinians, motivated by a sense of injustice, retreated further into their defensive shell, and the harder England tried to crack it, the more the opposition seemed to bond together. But as Moore was to point out, 'Martin and Geoff knew each other's play by instinct, and suddenly they found a chink of space that they'd used a million times for West Ham.' The goal, indeed, had West Ham written all over it – Peters laid in a near-post cross, and Hurst burst across the players marking him to apply the priceless finishing touch. 'That taught a lot of people the value of having the understanding of good club units in the England team,' Moore said.

*　　　*　　　*

Alan Shearer, the most highly acclaimed of the present group of British strikers, is very much a self-made scorer. He has got into the position he occupies today more through his strength of character, his capacity for hard work and his positive attitude than natural ability. Indeed, those who have been associated with him during his rise to the top are agreed that he is the perfect example of a footballer who has got the absolute maximum out of himself.

The other reason why Shearer attracts so much praise is that, for all the success and adulation, he remains as level-headed and self-effacing now as he was when he started his career. 'He is a superstar, but he doesn't have a superstar's ego,' says his former Blackburn coach and manager, Ray Harford. In other words, Shearer remains ever-willing to adjust to any job he is given, and has no compunction about sacrificing his individuality in the best interests of his team.

Most great 'leaders' of teams can be found at the back. But Shearer, a man with an unrivalled ability to rescue seemingly lost causes, is one of the few who can lift a side equally effectively from the front. This is why Newcastle paid a then world record transfer fee of £15 million for him and he has been appointed England captain. At a time when English football has become big business, with the money being paid to the top performers having gone through the proverbial roof, it also helps explain why Shearer, at 27, has become a millionaire.

All of which must make Geoff Hurst wonder what life would be like for him if he were playing for West Ham and England now. Of all the former players who would have been ideal for the present Premiership scene, the credentials of Hurst – the Alan Shearer of his day – seem particularly compelling.

In addition to the amount of running he got through off the ball to create space for his colleagues, Hurst scored 248 goals in 499 West Ham matches, plus 24 in 49 England games. In that department, the performance for which he is best remembered – outside that World Cup final hat-trick – was in West Ham's First Division match at home to Sunderland on 19 October 1968. The Hammers had beaten Sunderland 5–1 at Roker Park 12 months earlier, yet this could hardly have helped prepare them for the shock of what happened to them when Hurst and West Ham really did get the bit between the teeth against their relegation-threatened team.

West Ham won 8–0 – and Hurst got six.

The only occasion that West Ham have ever registered such a big league win was on 8 March 1958, when Rotherham were thrashed 8–0 in a Second Division fixture. Their leading marksman that day was their Scottish striker Johnny Dick, and the other goals came from John Smith and Vic Keeble, both of whom scored twice.

When Hurst went to work on that demolition job on Sunderland, the other scorers were Moore and Trevor Brooking. The other members of the West Ham team that day were Bobby Ferguson, Billy Bonds, Alan Stephenson, Gary Charles, Martin Peters, Ronnie Boyce, Harry Redknapp and Johnny Sissons. It is pertinent to mention them all because, although it was Hurst who put himself in the top of the spot, the service he received from the supporting cast was something that a lot of fellow strikers spend all their careers just fantasising about.

Jim Montgomery, Sunderland goalkeeper, recalls: 'I actually won the man of the match award in some of the papers the next day, which shows you what the score could have been.

'You could say that it was one of those days when everything West Ham tried came off – Geoff even got one with a shot from outside the box. All teams like to think that they are capable of giving a side a real hiding, but this was always liable to happen with a team as committed to attack and as skilful as West Ham were. The quality of their passing and build-up play, especially when they got the ball on to the flanks for Redknapp and Sissons, was superb. The man in our team that I felt sorry for was big Charlie Hurley [Sunderland's centre-half]. Geoff Hurst gave him a terrible time – West Ham were pulling us all over the place and when the final ball went in, Charlie just couldn't cope with Geoff's movement.

'Whenever the ball came into the box from the right or left wing, Geoff would time his run to perfection to get in front of him. He did it time and time again.'

Hurley, it should be remembered, was no mug. An established Irish Republic international, he had been looked upon as the most skilful centre-half in Britain. The members of the West German defence who conceded those three Hurst goals in the World Cup final were no mugs either.

If there was one goal which summed up what Hurst was all about, it was England's fourth in the last minute, from a long pass by Moore. 'It was another West Ham job,' Moore said. 'I couldn't count how many times I had knocked that same pass into the that same space for Geoff to make that same run. They [the Germans] were shattered and it split them wide open. Geoff was exhausted too, but he was stronger than them.' Thus, Hurst elected to head straight for goal, ignoring the tiredness in his limbs in his quest to either get in a scoring shot, or at least get the ball far enough away from the England half to deny the Germans the time to make it 3–3.

He himself has said: 'I really did not care if I missed, as long as the ball went a long way back up the terraces, out of harm's way.'

So Hurst, by now virtually on his knees, hit the ball with every ounce of power he could muster – and Wembley exploded as it curved into the top of the net.

For England's centre-half, Jack Charlton, one of the most vivid memories of that goal concerned his screams at Moore, as the England captain had gained possession and then settled on the ball to work out his best passing option. Charlton, mindful of the Germans' ability to punish their opponents' mistakes, says: 'I just wanted Bobby to belt the ball up the field – anywhere. I was screaming at him: "Bobby, get it clear . . . get rid of it." Then, when he played that pass to Hurst and Hurst scored, I thought: "I'm never going to be able to play this effing game."'

When Moore, Peters and Hurst were at their pomp for West Ham, how many other rival players were moved to take that view of themselves?

CHAPTER 3

Billy Bonds

Billy Bonds once suffered a horrific-looking nose injury during a five-a-side training match, but as the West Ham physiotherapist, Rob Jenkins, attempted to stem the flow of blood, the only thing on the player's mind seemed to be whether it would put him out of action for the Hammers' First Division match the following day.

'I've got to play, Rob,' Bonds muttered. 'Can you patch me up?'

'Bill,' Jenkins replied wearily. 'Don't be a f***ing hero.'

It was not the most pertinent piece of advice that could have been offered to Bonds for the simple reason that being a hero was second nature to him.

You start to get the picture when you raise the subject of Alan Shearer with him. 'He is very tough, mentally tough,' Bonds enthuses. 'As soon as things start getting a bit hard, some players pack it in. Their bodies send signals to the brain, and the brain goes: "Oh, switch off, bang." But with him, it won't.' So does not Bonds look upon him as a kindred spirit? 'Well, yeah, that's right. You lock in, don't you? I mean, I used to love a physical challenge. There was no better feeling than that of battling with people to the point where they became deflated. I loved that side of the game.'

Hence the fact that never has there been a more inspiring figure in British football than Billy Bonds MBE. Never has there been a man who has given a club better service and the fans greater value for their money than he did at Upton Park. When it comes to automatic choices for this West Ham dream team, it is not unreasonable to suggest that Bonds, who did not gain one cap for England, would be as difficult to leave out as even Moore, Peters and Hurst.

Born and raised in Woolwich, south London, and bought by the Hammers from Charlton for £49,500 in 1967 at the age of 21, Bonzo spent 27 years with the club as player, coach and then manager. During his 21-season career there as a player, his achievements included a record 793 first-team appearances (including 663 in the league); emulating Moore's feat of being voted the supporters' 'Hammer of the Year' as many as four times; and succeeding Moore as captain.

The choice of Bonds to lead the team in 1974 was tantamount to jumping from one extreme to another. He was as physical and assertive as Moore was technically sophisticated and laid-back. 'Bobby and I were like chalk and cheese,' he acknowledges. 'He would lead by example, whereas I would shake my fist and bawl at people, even threaten them. I don't think Bobby Moore ever threatened anyone in his life. I wasn't the prettiest sight on a football field – unlike him, you could never say that I had an elegant style of play. How could you liken me to someone like Bobby? In fact, I don't think I was like anybody really. All you could say about me was that I got the job done.'

In his way, though, the example Bonds set was no less valuable than Moore's. His boundless energy, enthusiasm and spirit – which saw him still playing in the old First Division when he was 41, and still pushing himself beyond the limits imposed by many younger players – were qualities that would have been worth their weight in gold to any club in any era. His Peter Pan persona attracted the attention of sports enthusiasts even in the United States, a country in which professional soccer is no more than a minority spectator sport compared to American football, baseball and basketball. The *New York Times* ran a profile of Bonds, and NBC, one of the major American TV sports networks, produced a documentary about him. Those who worked with Bonds, not to mention those who played against him, left no superlative unused in their attempts to convey their admiration for him. 'He just keeps amazing me,' said West Ham manager John Lyall. 'He is the nearest thing I have seen to a football machine. He just goes on and on.' Indeed, Billy Bonds in action, bursting up and down the pitch, ever-hungry to be involved, was a sight to behold. So, too, was his level of consistency.

His late father, Arthur, who worked in the maintenance department of London Transport, didn't waste words when he felt that his son had been below par. 'One to forget today, son,' he would tell him. Yet, as reflected by the number of times his West Ham managers selected him, his bad days were sufficiently rare for him to be left scratching his head in striving to think of any examples.

The words 'one to forget today, son' were certainly appropriate in connection with a Bonds mistake in an opening match of the season against Wrexham. He himself still shakes his head at the memory of an opponent beating him to a throw-out from West Ham keeper Phil Parkes near the end – courtesy of Bonds waiting for the ball to arrive at his feet – and scoring the only goal. 'But the amazing thing about that game was that I had been playing a blinder up to then,' he says.

An even worse nightmare for him was his sending off – with Colin Todd – for fighting in a vital Second Division promotion clash with Birmingham City at Upton Park in March 1980. Bonds' rush of blood to the head, with the score at 1–1, contributed to a 2–1 West Ham defeat which destroyed the Hammers' faint chance of getting back into the First Division that season; and coming six days after their FA Cup semi-final victory over Everton, it could easily have caused him to miss the honour of being one of the few captains to have led a team in two finals. 'Billy, who was an experienced professional, was ashamed of himself afterwards,' John Lyall recalled. 'He should have known better. As he sat in the dressing-room, the full implications of his actions began to dawn on him. The FA Cup final – a big London derby against Arsenal – was less than three weeks away. The Football Association suspension would almost certainly rule him out of the big day.'

Fortunately, Bonds did make the Wembley party because West Ham appealed against the sending off and the FA, noting his improved disciplinary record since his early days, were persuaded to view the automatic one-match suspension he had already served as sufficient punishment. Bonds' sense of relief then was nothing compared to what it was like when West Ham beat Arsenal 1–0, thus giving him another winner's medal to put alongside the one he gained when West Ham beat Fulham in the final in 1975.

The only other 'one to forget' that springs to his mind was the 3–3 draw at home to West Bromwich Albion in November 1977. Ron Greenwood, then England manager, had included him in the national squad – for the first time – for that month's 1978 World Cup qualifying tie against Italy at Wembley, and Bonds recalls: 'All the Italian papers reckoned I would be in the team to do a man-for-man marking job on one of their top players and the speculation increased when Ron came down to watch the West Bromwich Albion game. Now Ron knew what I could do better than anybody – whatever I was going to do that day was not going to make any difference to my chances of his putting me in the England team.

'But for some reason, I was nervous. I'm thinking: "Bloody heck, Ron's up there [in the stand] watching me – I've got a chance to play for England." Well, I had a stinker – not a stinker, maybe, but a poor game by my standards. I was edgy; I was trying to do things I would not have done normally, complicating my game a little bit.

'This just wasn't me. My game was all about keeping it simple.'

That summed him up as a person, too. Off the field as well as on it, Bonds was refreshingly straightforward and open. In some ways, there was more to him than met the eye. Off the field, he relaxed with long walks in the country and reading the works of Thomas Hardy – hardly the sort of interests you might have expected of a man with his social background and blood-and-thunder football style. But as far as his football career was concerned, what you saw was what you got – and he has not changed. Today, quite apart from our memories of him as a player, it is also possible to get the full flavour of him when listening to him talk.

Here's how Bonds, now Millwall's manager, looks back on his long West Ham playing record: 'I just loved it, every minute of it. The training and the playing . . . it's all I ever wanted to do.

'The West Ham crowd probably just saw me as a ball-winner, a wholehearted player all sweat and blood and thunder, and that was it. I feel I was a lot more than that, but nevertheless the enthusiasm I had was definitely a big part of my game and helped me win the crowd over straight away. When I'm talking to young players now, I always stress that people want to see professional footballers who have a bit of enthusiasm, who look as if they are enjoying it and are prepared to give 100 per cent. I say: "If people see you doing that, then they'll get behind you. If you can add little things to your game, so much the better. But the enthusiasm's got to be there first of all."

'I was fortunate inasmuch as I only had a couple of what you would call bad injuries. The first one was a groin problem which came just before the 1975 FA Cup final against Fulham. I played virtually on one leg that day and immediately afterwards I had an operation [which kept him out of the Hammers' line up for the first half of the following season]. Then, ten years later, I had knee ligament damage followed by two operations on the small toe of my left foot [part of the toe was amputated because of an infected bone, and he missed the whole of the 1985–86 season]. But that was about it really.

'I suppose I was also lucky in being what you might call a naturally fit person,' Bonds continues. 'I mean, as a professional footballer I ate what most experts would tell you are the wrong things. I loved the beer, and before a game it was not unusual for me to eat two fillet steaks – Trevor Brooking had a habit of leaving his portion, and I would go and nick it sort of thing. Dieticians involved with sport now argue that you should never have red meat before a game – it should be pasta and rice – but I kept fuelling myself in that way all my life. At home anything the wife put on the table for me, I'd eat. I loved it. I didn't really have any fads about anything – you know, I was a very uncomplicated person.

'I don't know, when you talk about my fitness and strength, I would suggest that perhaps my background had something to do with it. The thing I remember the most about my childhood is that I was so active. As a kid, I used to go out a lot with my father. We never had a car, and because he was such a big bloke – six foot one – I always seemed to be running to keep up with him. I used to run everywhere – I ran to school, I ran up the High Street when I was doing errands for my parents, I was always on the go. I had a bicycle when I got older, and loved going off on long runs into the countryside. I was never just sitting around, watching TV or videos, or listening to music.

'But I still keep coming back to that word "enthusiasm". As far as I am concerned, that's the base for everything. Once you get into your 30s, people can easily talk you out of it. "What are you going to do now?" they say. But every year, when I reported back for pre-season training, I just felt so good. My age wasn't something I was concerned about because I knew what I could do. I knew I could still compete with the younger players, and I knew that I still had bags of enthusiasm for it. Even at 40, I was still doing exactly the same training that I had been doing when I was 19. I remember reading somewhere that once Bobby Charlton got into his 30s, he had started to ease up on his training, but I believed that you should train as you play on the Saturday. If anything, I probably worked myself even harder when I got beyond that age.

'I'll be honest with you, I really think I could have gone on for another couple of years, certainly at a lower level if not at West Ham. When you reach a certain age, there aren't many periods in which you can say you are 100 per cent fit – you always seem to be carrying a little knock and you do start to feel more tired after matches, but you just put it to the back of your mind. However, when I got to 39 or 40, the strain was causing me to lose a bit of weight, and it eventually got to the stage where my missus kept telling me how gaunt I looked. So that's when I thought: "Well, maybe I'll pack it in now." The other reason I retired as a player then was that I couldn't bear the thought of lowering my standards. It would have been easy for me to go down the scale, but I knew that I could easily look crap in a lesser team. The last thing I wanted was people looking at me in their team, and saying: "What's that old so-and-so doing there?"'

One of the most interesting things about Bonds as a player was that, outside training and playing, he was not one to spend a lot of time with his dressing-room colleagues. One West Ham player was quoted as saying 'Billy is rarely seen in the players' bar at Upton Park – I doubt whether he even knows where it is.' Bonds continued to live south of the river, close to his Woolwich roots – in Chislehurst, Kent – and could usually be relied upon to be the first to get changed and depart for home. 'I got on great with all the players – I don't think I ever had one enemy in the West Ham dressing-room – but as far as I was concerned, we saw enough of each other in work every day. That was good enough for me. I did not feel the need to socialise with them. For example, I got on particularly well with Trevor Brooking, but outside our football commitments, I never had one night out with Trevor. The thing was, I had a family, and when I wasn't working, I wanted to be with them.'

Nor did Bonds ever feel the need to join a bigger club, and so improve his bank balance. Professional football is a relatively short, unpredictable career and as the power and status of the leading players has increased – following the abolition of the maximum wage, the introduction of freedom of contract and, most recently, the Jean-Marc Bosman ruling – the sort of loyalty that Bonds showed to West Ham has inevitably become rarer. Today, at a time when so many top-class players are coming across as money-grabbing opportunists, Bonds' recollections of his contentment with his West Ham lot seem almost quaint.

'To this day, I have no idea if any clubs came in for when I was with West Ham because I never asked. It never bothered me, I really mean that.

'Perhaps the biggest regret about my West Ham career was

that I did not get an England cap. It would be nice to say now that I played for England – I am not being conceited, but I think I was a lot better than some of the other players who have won caps. The closest I got was when Ron [Greenwood] selected me as a substitute for the Italy game [the home World Cup qualifying tie in 1978] – very frustrating because I thought Ron could have got me on [with England leading 2–0], but I was left on the bench.'

He did not even get that far on the two other occasions he was in the England squad, for matches against Germany and Brazil. He had to withdraw from the first one because of a calf injury, and from the second because of cracked ribs – ironically sustained as the result of a collision with West Ham goalkeeper Phil Parkes.

'So I cannot say that I got the most out of myself at West Ham,' he says, 'but nor can I say that I regretted being there for so long. I wouldn't change a thing because, who knows, things could easily have gone the other way for me. It's hypothetical, isn't it? It doesn't matter really, because I enjoyed every minute of it and that's the most important thing.

'I was happy about where I lived, the fact that the kids were settled, and things like that were all that mattered me. It sounds funny now – a bit naïve – but it's the truth. Not once did I want to leave the club, even though I was not among the highest-paid players there. I know for a fact that other players got more than me, but again, I was contented because money was not the thing that motivated me.

'I think it's important to be true to yourself. You get some people who, once they get a few bob, tend to forget where they have come from and who they are. I have never done that. My roots are important to me and my family are important to me. Although I probably could have doubled my wages going somewhere else, I felt that I was already earning enough. I did not want to drag my family all over the shop, you see. I'd got a lovely home, the kids were at private schools – what else did I need?

'I remember the times when I went in to see the gaffer [Ron

Greenwood] about my contract during the early part of my West Ham career. You couldn't just walk in to the manager's office when you wanted then, you had to make an appointment, and an hour or two before I was due to see him, I would be quite apprehensive about it. I'd be thinking: "Oh, Christ – I don't want to do this." Anyway, you'd walk in to his lovely office and he'd say, "Right, I'm going to give you a £50-a-week rise, and a two-year contract with a one-year option," and that would be that. I'd just say, "Oh thanks, Mr Greenwood," and then go home to the missus and tell her that we'd got a bit of security for the next couple of years. That's the way it was then – there were no agents then, nobody to advise you, and in the main you accepted what was offered to you.

'Even when all this began to change, I should imagine that I was the easiest of players to deal with. I wasn't too bothered about getting money from outside sources either, from things like TV and personal appearances. People used to say, "Oh, he's shy." It wasn't that; it was just that I didn't want to do it. When I wasn't training or playing, I didn't want to be dashing off here and there. I didn't want to complicate my life. The more uncomplicated my life, the more I could concentrate on my football and enjoy it.'

That his link with West Ham was so powerful might have been viewed as surprising, given his upbringing south of the Thames, and the long allegiances of his father and himself to Millwall and Charlton respectively. West Ham, on the other side of the Blackwall Tunnel, might just as well have been situated on a different planet. Indeed, until his transfer to West Ham, at the age of 19, Bonds had been to Upton Park twice. His first trip there came at the age of 14, when the Sunday League team he played for was taken by their manager to see a West Ham match against Burnley, as a Guy Fawkes Night treat. Bonds still remembers the glow of Burnley's football, let alone that of the bonfires and fireworks. Burnley, who were then one of the most talked-about teams in the country and had the brilliant Irish international inside-forward Jimmy McIlroy playing for them, won 5–2. It was not until three years later, when Bonds was a

17-year-old Charlton youth team player, that he returned – this time for a match against West Bromwich Albion. Again, as one would expect of a match involving West Ham, there was no lack of scoring excitement for the young Bonds, with Brian Dear hitting five goals in a 6–0 Hammers victory.

'There are some teams you wouldn't cross the road to see, but as a neutral, West Ham were always among the two or three in London that you didn't mind going to,' Bonds says. 'You knew that you would see a football match, an entertaining game.'

Nonetheless, before he joined West Ham, Bonds only had eyes for his beloved Charlton. 'West Ham was a club I never really thought about,' he admits, and even when Charlton agreed to sell him to the Hammers, Bonds' reaction was less than ecstatic. He recalls: 'I will never forget the night that Bob Stokoe [Charlton's manager then] pulled me into his office to discuss the transfer with Ron.

'It was immediately after a match against Birmingham, and I apparently gave off the wrong vibes to Ron straight away by saying: "Look, Mr Greenwood, I think Sunderland and Leicester are also in for me." At that, Ron blanked me, totally blanked me. So I went out the room and a few minutes later Bob Stokoe came to me and says: "You've really upset him. He's really disappointed that you mentioned Sunderland and Leicester – get back in there and tell him that West Ham are the club you want to sign for." The rest is history . . .'

Part of that history is that West Ham were able to help Bonds become a better footballer without detracting in any way from his real strengths. He joined the club as a right-back, and as he says: 'In those days I was exceptionally raw – the main thing I had going for me was a good pair of lungs – and Ron and John [Lyall] added a lot to my game in terms of passing and movement and things like that.

'I was also lucky to play with so many top-class players. There is nothing better for youngsters than to have someone in the first-team who can make them think: "I want to be like him . . . I want to do what he can do." I had examples like Bobby Moore, Martin Peters, Geoff Hurst, Ronnie Boyce – all great players who helped and encouraged me.

'But Ron was remarkable in that respect.

'A lot of managers and coaches nowadays are putting on training sessions designed to improve their players' movement off the ball and passing, and they're saying that the ideas are new. But they are not new to me because we were actually doing the same sort of stuff under Ron's management at West Ham when I first went there 30 years ago. People tended to laugh at West Ham then because the club's reputation for being more advanced than others in their coaching and training ideas was not borne out by their Championship record. This was a bit unfair on Ron because, in my time at West Ham, we suffered to a great extent by not having the money that the big north of England clubs and London clubs like Tottenham and Arsenal had, so in terms of strength in depth we were always a couple of quality players short of being able to produce a title-winning team.

'At the same time, I don't think anyone fancied playing West Ham because the one thing that Ron always insisted upon – and it was something that John Lyall [his successor as manager] carried on – was that the players had to express themselves. John was probably a better motivator than Ron and put a greater emphasis on defensive organisation, but John had learned almost everything he knew about the game from Ron, so his basic ideas on how it should be played were quite similar.

'Ron just encouraged people to go out and play. His attitude was that if the opposition scored three goals, we were capable of getting four. Most of our work in training was devoted to how we could break teams down and I was never really coached on the defensive side of the game. Even as a right-back or a central defender, if I wanted to bomb forward – well, Ron would encourage that all the time. It amuses me sometimes when people ask me what it was like to be a defender in such an attack-minded team, in a team where the men at the back did not get as much protection as the defenders in other sides. I attacked as much as anybody else.

'As a full-back, I'd go missing a lot. I thought nothing of going forward, beyond our winger, and getting into the box – that was the way Ron liked it.'

So much so that even against the team Bonds least relished playing against – Don Revie's brilliant but ruthless Leeds United – he was able to adopt a positive attitude. It says much about West Ham's attacking ability under Greenwood that in November 1966, the year before Bonds' arrival at Upton Park, the Hammers inflicted upon Leeds one of the biggest defeats in the Yorkshire club's history – a 7–0 thrashing in the League Cup.

As for Bonds' own performances against Leeds, and especially those at right-back, he recalls: 'Leeds were one of the best sides I ever played against. They had everything – they had great individual players, were well organised and they could be as nasty as you like.

'You not only had Eddie Gray [the Leeds outside-left] to worry about down that left side, but also Terry Cooper [the left-back] – and Cooper was as good going forward as Gray was. I remember Ron saying to Harry Redknapp [West Ham's outside-right]: "Get at him – he can't defend." But Harry couldn't get near him, he couldn't get enough of the ball in their own half to do it and it ended up with Cooper repeatedly taking me on at the other end. You were not frightened of players like that, however. It was a challenge, and in every way I think I gave as good as I got against them.

'I'm sure this is one of the reasons why Ron shoved me into midfield. He did need more of a defensive backbone in there; he had plenty of players who could use the ball, but I was one of the few who could win it. The other reason, though, was that he knew I had the energy to do the ball-winning job and also get into the box. Oh, I loved it – it was so enjoyable to be given that freedom.'

Never more so than in the 1973–74 season, when Bonds made a typically stirring contribution to the Hammers' battle to stay in the First Division by emerging as their top league scorer with 13 goals, only three of which came from penalties. His best scoring achievement was in March, when he got all three in a 3–0 home win over Chelsea. He also found the net against

Manchester United (2), Coventry (2), Ipswich, QPR, Sheffield United, Arsenal, Everton and Derby.

He recalls: 'Around that time, when I was in my late 20s, I was probably playing the best football of my career. All players have what they call golden spells, and that was mine. I was a bit wild in my younger days at West Ham and I think it was at that stage that I started to mature and think a little more about the game. Also, I felt so good physically, so strong and powerful, and everything seemed to be coming off for me.'

The spell in which he scored that hat-trick against Chelsea summed it up perfectly. Before the game he was presented with no fewer than three newspaper player of the month awards comprising bottles of champagne, silver salvers and a statuette. As he says: 'To then go out and get the first hat-trick of my career – well.' Two of his goals came through his ability to latch on to loose balls in and around the six-yard box, from shots by Clyde Best and Graham Paddon that Chelsea's keeper, John Phillips, managed to get to but failed to hold. He was particularly pleased with the other, when he climbed above Ron Harris by the far post to head in a Paddon cross.

He could easily have had another hat-trick in the next match against Coventry (when he scored two goals including a penalty in a 3–2 West Ham defeat); and this was followed by his scoring again in the 1–1 draw against Derby. 'In the match against Derby, I burst into the box to get on the end of a cross, and happened to catch the ball with my ear,' he recalls, laughing. 'But it went into the net, and the next day one newspaper said: "The marauding Bonds scored West Ham's goal with a glancing header." That shows you what sort of season it was for me – I couldn't go wrong.'

That was not the only period when West Ham had good cause to be thankful for Bonds' spirit in adversity, his relish of back-to-the-wall situations. Regular West Ham watchers will readily confirm that whenever their team were in trouble – a quite common occurrence in the league – Bonzo could always be relied upon to push himself to the front line in their battle to survive. One of his most famous performances was in May 1985, when the then 38-year-old East End cult figure pushed himself relentlessly through an Upton Park quagmire to inspire a 5–1 win over bottom-of-the-table Stoke – a success that ensured the Hammers' First Division safety with two matches left. Bonds scored twice, and also gained the penalty from which West Ham got one of their other goals.

Little wonder, therefore, that when John Lyall was sacked as manager in May 1989, Bonds (then the Hammers' youth team coach) was the 'people's choice' to succeed him; and that when he did eventually land the job in February 1990 – amidst the turmoil of a 6–0 League Cup semi-final defeat by Oldham and Lou Macari's resignation as a result of his involvement in a betting scandal concerning his previous club, Swindon – the sense of relief and elation was overwhelming.

With West Ham in the Second Division, Bonds, never one to try to kid anyone through the language of diplomacy, was characteristically straightforward on the subject of what his team needed to lift itself back to the top. 'They call this place "The Academy", but that stuff has been overplayed,' he said. 'Sure I like to see West Ham play attractive, attacking football, but sometimes you have to roll up your sleeves and get stuck in.' Fair enough, but as Bonds was to discover, his life as a manager – with all its countless different aspects and imponderables – was far different from the comparatively narrow-minded existence he had been able to create for himself as a player. Uncomplicated it wasn't – as can be deduced from the roller-coaster ride he experienced in the West Ham job.

After finishing the 1989–90 season just outside the Second Division play-off zone, West Ham were promoted to the top flight in 1991, relegated in 1992 (in a season when Bonds and his troops could not have been helped by the fans' angry demonstrations against the board over the club's ill-conceived Bond scheme), and then promoted again in 1993. Ironically, at the start of the 1993–94 campaign, there was some animosity towards Bonds himself when he sold Julian Dicks – almost as big a cult figure among West Ham followers as he had been as a player – to Liverpool for £1.5 million. But anyone who knew

Bonds could not have been surprised that the Hammers went on to confound the bookmakers by keeping their heads above relegation water, and that when Bonds parted company with the club at the start of the following season, the general reaction was one of shock and dismay.

The background to this parting of the ways provided one of the biggest controversies in the club's history. West Ham just stated that Bonds had resigned. But Bonds, clearly anxious to dispel the impression of him as just another manager who had found the pressures of the job too much for him, revealed that the board had wanted Harry Redknapp (who Bonds had brought back to the club as his right-hand man) to take over from him as manager: 'I had a meeting with the chairman and he told me they wanted to shuffle things around. They wanted Harry as manager and they wanted me to become a paid director. I did not fancy that . . . I was not ready to go upstairs.'

Following stints on the backroom staff of QPR and Reading, Bonds returned to the manager's job at Millwall in the summer of 1997 and, after what happened to him at West Ham, might well feel that he has a point to prove. Only time will tell to what extent his departure from the manager's office at Upton Park was a loss to the club, but the one thing we can be sure about is that they would relish the opportunity to turn back the clock and have him there now as a player – providing the West Ham dream team would release him, of course.

CHAPTER 4

Phil Parkes

Such is West Ham's age-old reputation for putting their attacking instincts above all else, any of their goalkeepers might well have been expected to take the field with a government health warning stamped on his gloves. Anyone, that is, except Phil Parkes.

There was something quite reassuring about the sight of the amiable Midlands giant in the Hammers goal, not least because Parkes – six foot three and 15 stone – was one of the last people at Upton Park who could be expected to get angry over the adventurous spirit and defensive indiscipline of the players in front of him.

The only time the disconcertingly laid-back Parkes can ever recall having a row with anyone at Upton Park, it was with the coach, Mick McGivern, during a five-a-side training match. McGivern, the referee, awarded a goal against Parkes, following a shot which the keeper knew had hit the post. 'He just did it to wind us up,' says Parkes. 'He did it all the time, but on this occasion, I rose to the bait, I'm afraid. "You always effing do this," I said. "Every Friday afternoon, you come in here and spoil things." With that, I just walked off. "Where are you going?" he asked. "I am going to get changed before I hit you," I said.' The other players were gobsmacked – this was not the placid, quiet-spoken keeper they knew and loved. 'I reckon they thought: "God – must be PMT or something."' True, he broke Billy Bonds' ribs, Paul Allen's ankle, Alvin Martin's collar bone and knocked out Tony Gale – but these were merely the result of these gentlemen happening to be in Parkes' way when he came off his line to collect the ball. 'They knew the score, if they were in the way, they were going to get hit. They only did it once.'

Some opponents did make the mistake of riling him, but even then he always seemed in perfect control of his emotions. In that respect, he shows you a scar down a shin and recalls that it was inflicted by little Terry Gibson, the former Tottenham striker then playing against the Hammers for Manchester United. 'I've come out, got the ball – and then suddenly little Terry has come right over the top of me,' Parkes explains. As Parkes was clambering to his feet, he was seen to smile broadly at Gibson and the two even appeared to exchange pleasantries. Indeed, one newspaper the following day, referring to the fact that United's goalkeeper, Gary Bailey, had 'made a meal' of an earlier challenge on him by Frank McAvennie, praised Parkes for his calm, sporting reaction.

The writer clearly couldn't lip-read. 'While I was smiling at Terry,' Parkes says, 'I was saying to him "Do that again, you little b*****d and I'll break your f***ing leg."'

It seems surprising that he didn't threaten this more often – to the members of his own team. All goalkeepers like to think they will get some protection from their colleagues, even those at the front, in terms of their making it difficult for the opposition to get in shots and headers. As managers and coaches keep telling us: 'Not conceding goals, like scoring them, should be a collective responsibility.' Parkes, though, got less protection than most. Indeed, the only consolation for him was that it could have been worse; at least he wasn't playing for a West Ham team under the management of Ron Greenwood. Bobby Moore, addressing the question of West Ham's defensive vulnerability under Greenwood through what they did (or didn't do) when the other team gained possession, once said: 'One of the problems was that sometimes West Ham didn't work hard enough at denying the opposition time and space on the ball. They were so obsessed with creating space for themselves that they could not or did not recover when moves broke down.'

West Ham's England midfield star Trevor Brooking, in his 1981 autobiography, said: 'During his time at West Ham, Ron had to strive to achieve some kind of balance between sticking to his attacking beliefs and getting results. When the team were not playing well, the temptation was there to pull more players back and tighten up defensively, which most managers would have done. He refused to do this. In the years when we were fighting relegation, we were still encouraged to attack. We were criticised for being too slack defensively and that was probably true. Ron's forte was working with expressive attacking players.

'I have never known him to say before a match: "We'll have to play this one tight and aim for a draw", not even when West Ham have been playing at Anfield or Old Trafford. His team-talk was always about trying to win, about being positive and scoring goals.'

As Brooking said, the principles of Greenwood's successor, John Lyall, were slightly different. 'He wants flair in attack, but he also wants consistency in defence, which is why he changed the staff round two years ago and brought in players like Phil Parkes, Ray Stewart, Alvin Martin and Paul Allen. The change was noticed more away from home than at home. Whereas before we might go to Preston or Blackburn and impress people with our attacking ability as we lost, we would now go to places like that and battle for a 0–0 draw if that was the best result we could achieve on the day. The joke at Upton Park is that John Lyall has put steel rods up our backs.'

Old habits can die hard, however, especially for a club with West Ham's deeply ingrained traditions. So when his team did revert to their old selves, it was just as well that Lyall had Parkes to get them out of difficulties.

It was a bonus that Lyall and West Ham were to enjoy for 12 years, in which time Parkes made 436 first-team appearances (344 in the league). Parkes and Lyall had immense respect for each other both as professionals and as people. Hence the fact that when Lyall became Ipswich manager in 1990, he enlisted Parkes as the club's part-time goalkeeping coach; and that during Parkes' 40th birthday party at home on 8 August 1990,

Lyall – whom Parkes believed to be on club business in the north of England – took delight in making himself a surprise guest.

'Strangely enough, when he came through that door, it was the only time that I called him "Boss",' Parkes says. 'I knew that I was going to get on with this guy from the day that he sat in my home and asked me to sign for West Ham. We just chatted like you and I are chatting now, and as a player under him, I never referred to him as anything but "John". I don't think anyone ever called him "Boss". That's the sort of person he was.'

That West Ham elected to part company with Lyall in the summer of 1989, following the club's relegation from the First Division, was somewhat embarrassing to Parkes because many felt that the manager had brought it upon himself by not using the keeper as much as he should have done.

Lyall's attitude to him as a regular first-team player then was influenced not just by Parkes' age, but also the serious elbow infection that had ended his run in the side towards the end of the 1986–87 season. Parkes, who had to undergo surgery on the elbow tendons, made only one appearance the following season (when Tom McAllister became a first-team regular) and at the start of the 1988–89 season he was pushed even further down the pecking order when Lyall bought the Irish keeper, Allen McKnight, from Celtic. This proved a disaster for the Hammers, with McKnight making costly mistakes and inevitably becoming the number-one target for abuse from the crowd.

But it was not until February that Lyall recalled the then 39-year-old Parkes to the side – a move that made a big enough difference to West Ham's goals-against record to invite the view that the Hammers might not have been relegated had the veteran been introduced earlier. Parkes says: 'I thought I could do the job. I never said anything – I could hardly come out and say "Look, I'm the one you should be playing" – but I was playing in the reserves and as far as I was concerned, I was ready to go in at any time.

'The thing is, I can't criticise John because he was genuinely trying to protect me. I think he was worried that I might not live up to the standards I had set in the past and get slaughtered, a bit like a boxer who takes on one fight too many and ends up being humiliated.'

In terms of their credibility, one wonders how many times Parkes protected West Ham. Lyall had to pay as much as £565,000 (a world record transfer fee for a keeper) to sign him from QPR in February 1979 – a deal that threatened to create a revolt by the relegation-threatened players Parkes left behind at Loftus Road. That in itself was some compliment to a player who had not come into the Football League – with Walsall – until the age of 19 and had previously combined playing non-league football for Brierley Hill with working as a carpenter. Only the day before Parkes' transfer to West Ham, Bob Wilson, then QPR's goalkeeping coach, had told him: 'It's really important that you stay on top of your game. This side [at QPR] are not very good, and you're going to be one of the mainstays in holding them together.'

Parkes recalls that when he went to Upton Park to finalise his personal terms and undergo his medical examination, the West Ham chairman, Reg Pratt, was so uptight about the prospect of QPR's chairman, Jim Gregory, changing his mind that Lyall advised him to take the keeper for a walk around the ground. Gregory in fact did throw a potential spanner in the works by insisting on all the money being paid 'up front', as opposed to the more normal practice in such big deals of the buying club handing over the cash in instalments. West Ham's reaction was 'Here's the cheque, Mr Gregory'.

'The funniest thing about the whole affair,' Parkes says, 'was that two days later, who should be conducting a BBC *Football Focus* interview with me on the transfer? Bob Wilson.'

The money West Ham spent on Parkes, an astronomical figure then, was soon justified.

The following season, the Hammers' remarkable FA Cup run, which culminated in their belying their Second Division status with a 1–0 win over Arsenal in the final, was ignited by the keeper's extraordinary show of defiance against West Bromwich Albion in the third round.

Parkes looks back on his performance in the 1–1 draw at The

Hawthorns as the best of his career. He says: 'I made quite a lot of saves that day – West Brom were all over us – but the one that really stands out in my mind was from a Gary Owen free-kick on the edge of the box. I read what he was going to do – bend it with his left foot – but as I've started to go, the ball takes a deflection and so I have suddenly got to readjust. The ball's going one way, I'm going another. I don't know how I did it – it was just an instinctive thing – but I managed to get a hand to the ball and tip it over. Gary Owen just came over to me and said: "I don't believe that."'

The save took place in the first half, and at half-time, West Ham were in the fortuitous position of being a goal ahead. 'Billy [Bonds] and I were having a pee,' Parkes recalls, 'and Billy said to me: "We're winning 1–0, but we should be at least six behind. You never know, our name could be on the Cup this year." Those were his very words.'

In the second half, Parkes continued in the same vein. Thus, though West Brom did manage to get the ball past him – thanks to Cyrille Regis – they ended up as demoralised as West Ham were jubilant. Indeed, it says much about the nature of Parkes' performance that at the final whistle West Brom's players, who were to lose 2–1 in the replay at Upton Park, all made a point of seeking him out to congratulate him. So, too, did West Brom's manager, Ron Atkinson. Parkes recalls: 'He came out of the dug-out, shook my hand, and said: "You bastard. That performance was 11 out of 10."'

Not long ago, the two men came face to face again at a Fantasy Football awards dinner, when Atkinson had the job of making the presentations and Parkes agreed to collect one of the trophies on behalf of the Leeds keeper Nigel Martyn. 'As I was approaching the platform, big Ron grabbed the microphone and told the audience about the West Brom tie. He said: "I have to say that this guy coming up here produced the greatest goalkeeping performance I have ever seen." It was nice.'

The advantages of having a keeper like Parkes were emphasised even more emphatically in the seasons when the Hammers had their greatest league success. In the 1980–81 campaign, for example, when they won the Second Division Championship by a record 13 points, only 29 goals were conceded and Parkes, who played in all 42 matches, established a club record of 22 clean sheets. Little wonder that he was voted 'Hammer of the Year' by the supporters. He was a similarly prominent figure in the team in the 1985–86 season, when they finished third in the First Division – the closest the club has ever come to winning the Championship.

This was not the first time that Parkes had experienced that agonising 'so-near-yet-so-far' Championship feeling; he'd had it at QPR, as a member of the team who finished runners-up to Liverpool – by just one point – in the 1975–76 Championship race. To Parkes, the individual movement and overall cohesion of that team (who were managed by Dave Sexton, and included Frank McLintock, Gerry Francis, John Hollins, Stan Bowles, Dave Thomas and Don Givens), made them the most impressive 'total' footballing side he has seen in England. 'It was a case of everyone suddenly gelling together,' he adds. 'But it only lasted for about two-thirds of a season and by the following season it had gone. The team started to break up, and for the rest of the time I was there we were always up against it. So you always had plenty to do.'

All of which brings us back to West Ham, and especially his early days there. One thing that quickly became apparent to him was that their approach to the game was not as regimented and organised as QPR's had been.

'At QPR the training and coaching was geared to working on the team as units,' says Parkes. 'Every day the back four and myself would have to work together on our positioning in relation to each other and things like that – we'd practise the same things over and over again and it wasn't long before it became really monotonous. But the good part of it is that we all knew what our responsibilties were and exactly what each other was going to do in any situation. At West Ham, I got the impression that a lot of the training consisted of small-sided matches, five-a-sides, where everybody could express themselves and sort of do what they wanted. I think that was reflected by the way West Ham played.

'My first game for West Ham was against Oldham. We won 3–0, but the strange thing about it for me was that I still had a lot to do. You had the right-back turning up on the left wing, the left-back turning up on the right wing – that's not unusual, I know, but the two of them doing it at the same time is. I think I said to someone afterwards "I've never played in a team with ten attacking players and no defenders before." You know, they all just used to go off and do their own thing.'

This was bound to put pressure on Parkes, given his status as the world's most expensive keeper, but as he says: 'I did not put that price on my head, so it did not make any difference to me whatsoever.' He says he was much more nervous when he started playing for Walsall as a teenager.

'Believe it or not, I made my début for them on 1 April [1969] – I was so uptight, I couldn't even tie my bootlaces. Another reason why I remember it is that I played quite well – we beat Mansfield 3–1 – and the local *Express and Star* described me the next day as a "new discovery". I remember thinking: "That's strange. I've been here for two years."

'I think you have to be a little bit nervous before every game. If there isn't any adrenalin, then you're complacent and you're going to make mistakes. Where I was fortunate was that the fans took to me. At West Ham, the way they got behind me was awesome.'

To his fellow players, the same could be said about Parkes' temperament and ability. Unlike a lot of top professional foot-ballers, and though as determined to succeed as anyone, Parkes appreciated that the game was not the be-all and end-all of life. One example of how much the game meant to him is that he still has the match programme of every game in which he played. Nonetheless, he has always had a wide range of interests outside football – as quickly becomes apparent when you notice the large number of books on all manner of different subjects that adorn his study at home. If he had not been a professional footballer, he says he would have liked to have been 'an ornithologist or zoologist'.

As a West Ham player, Parkes found that making practical use of his DIY expertise was a particularly good way for him to relax off the field: 'Not long after I signed for West Ham, I bought my house here [in Wokingham, Berkshire] and converted it into two flats myself. I would come home from training and I'd be working up in the rafters – jumping around and lifting things – until seven o'clock or eight o'clock at night. If John Lyall could have seen me, he'd have had kittens. It did not occur to me that I should conserve my energy, or that I might put a drill through my hand or something.

'I'm very laid-back in most aspects of life really. It's the same with what I am doing now [earning his living as a builder and decorator]. The customer knows that I might take a bit longer to do a job because I want to go and play in a charity golf match, and they have to accept that. If they don't, that's too bad.'

Not surprisingly, he is critical of goalkeepers who are 'too demonstrative'. He argues: 'I look at Peter Schmeichel [of Manchester United]. He's a good keeper, but for me, he gets worked up for nothing and makes some horrendous clangers at times because of it. When you get keepers shouting and scream-ing, I am sure that half the time it's due to nerves or that they're trying to cover up for a mistake they have made. I could never imagine David Seaman [Arsenal] getting as irate as Schmeichel does.'

It was for this reason that Pat Jennings, the former Arsenal and Ireland star, was the keeper Parkes respected the most during his own career. 'So unflappable. Great.'

Parkes acknowledges that it is important for keepers to communicate with their colleagues at the back, but as he says: 'I found there was a limit to how much you could help them in the verbal sense, especially when you were playing before a big crowd. When 30,000 people were packed into Upton Park, for example, the noise they made was deafening – you couldn't hear yourself talk so all the shouting you did really amounted to little more than going through the motions.'

When Parkes was called into action, the noise that emanated from the West Ham diehards' throats could often be the sound of disbelief. His agility was surprising for such a big man. This, combined with his long reach, made him a superb shot-stopper, especially when it came to dealing with shots close to his feet (a nightmare for all keepers of his build); and, of course, there were few problems for him when it came to challenging for crosses.

'We played a lot of football in the streets when I was a kid, and right from the word go, I seemed to have the ability to fall on the concrete without hurting myself. So I always ended up in goal, and the more opportunities I was given to dive about, the more I loved it.

'I was very lucky inasmuch as I have always had a tremendous degree of suppleness and flexibility in the back. A lot of keepers suffer from back problems, but I never have.'

His proved a broad back, too, especially during the periods in which the Hammers needed to be 'carried' by him in that 1980–81 Second Division Championship-winning season. Quite apart from his 22-match 'clean sheet' record, only in seven matches did he concede more than one goal and only in two of those games did he let in more than two.

'It was crazy,' he recalls. 'The first home match – the very first day of the season – we played Luton, who had been a bogey side to West Ham for years. It's 0–0 with about five minutes to go, and then there are three penalties – yes, three penalties – and we've got beat 2–1. I can remember thinking: "A great start to the season this is. If this is the way our luck is going to go, we're going to be struggling." But suddenly, things took off.' Luton beat West Ham again on 15 November (3–2). By that time, though, the Hammers had established an inspired run which had yielded 11 wins and four draws. They put together an even more impressive run after losing 3–0 to Parkes' old QPR colleagues on 26 December – one comprising 14 wins and four draws.

'We were playing great football and everybody knew what they were doing,' says Parkes. 'There were hardly any changes to the team. Players got niggling injuries, but because everything was going so well, no one wanted to drop out of the side.'

That things were going well for West Ham in defence reflected as much credit on Lyall as it did on Parkes. At around the time Parkes had been signed from QPR, Lyall promoted Alvin Martin

to the regular number 5 first-team spot in place of Tommy
Taylor, a move that was to lead to Martin establishing an
outstanding partnership with Billy Bonds in the middle. The
back four was given another boost six months later when right-
back Ray Stewart, a tough Scot noted for his strength and
intelligence in defence, was signed from Dundee United for
£430,000. The deal made Stewart, then 19, the most expensive
teenager in British football; but Lyall, determined to bring a
greater degree of solidarity to the West Ham team, came up with
an even more eye-catching signing in August 1980 by buying
striker Paul Goddard (Parkes' former QPR colleague) for a club
record fee of £800,000.

As far as the heart of the defence was concerned, Parkes says:
'Frank McLintock and David Webb, the central defenders at
QPR when I was there, made a good combination, but on their
form together in that 1980–81 season, Billy and Alvin had to be
the best I have ever played with.' However, as Parkes points out,
the defending of all successful teams starts from the front. He
cites the example of Liverpool when they had Ian Rush – a
striker who did so much running off the ball, when the other
team had it, that some coaches looked upon him as the side's
most effective defender, let alone goalscorer. So when you ask
Parkes to name the players who helped him achieve his shut-out
distinction in 1980–81, the men who get a particularly
enthusiastic mention include Goddard, who had no peers in the
art of operating as a target man (and providing an outlet for
team-mates at the back to take the pressure off themselves), and
his fellow striker David Cross.

Goddard and Cross scored 56 goals between them that
season, an outstanding record in view of the fact that they had
never previously played together; and even Geoff Hurst, a
constant pain in the backside to opposing defenders if ever there
was one, would have been proud to have expended the amount
of energy they did off the ball – Cross especially. As Lyall was to
point out, Cross, hard and uncompromising and inclined
occasionally to appear clumsy, wasn't in the 'traditional West
Ham mould' when they bought him from West Bromwich

Albion in December 1977 (for a then club record fee of £180,000). 'But over the years, his touch and control improved significantly,' Lyall added. Even as Cross became more polished, the one thing that did not change was what was in his heart and soul. 'From the moment of his début for us against his old club WBA in December 1977, he was a player who gave me everything,' Lyall has said. 'He made a lot of friends at West Ham.'

Parkes certainly felt a close affinity towards him. Recalling Cross's part in West Ham's 1980 FA Cup triumph over Arsenal, when Lyall caused much confusion among the Gunners' incongruously rigid back four by playing the striker up front on his own, he says, 'Crossy was a tremendous runner and he was chasing across their back line all day. He made it so difficult for any of their defenders to settle on the ball and use it constructively. He just kept running backward and forward, and from side to side, and putting whoever was on the ball under pressure.'

It was a similar story the following season. One of the reasons why Parkes still remembers Cross's contribution concerns the framed £5 note – autographed by the striker – on his study wall.

The story behind it concerned an early-season Lyall prediction that Cross, then with 16 goals under his belt already, could be relied upon to end up with at least 20. Cross disagreed, pointing out that he had never scored 20 before and that it was not unusual for him to start a season on fire, goal-wise, but then fade. So the two men agreed that Lyall would give Cross £5 for every goal he scored over 20, and that Cross would give him £5 for every goal under that mark. By the time West Ham were due to face Grimsby at Blundell Park on 11 April, Cross's total stood at 29; and Lyall, £45 down, came to another agreement with the striker – that he would give Cross £10 for every goal he scored over 30, and that Cross would have to hand £20 to him if he stuck on 29. Cross, who hadn't scored for three successive matches – including the 2–0 win at Bristol Rovers seven days earlier, when the Hammers clinched the title – got four in a 5–1 victory.

Upon being paid the £40 Lyall owed him immediately

afterwards, Cross handed £5 to each of the four players who had provided the passes for his goals.

Among these was Parkes, who had set up the first for him with a massive clearance over the opposing centre-half.

Another present from Cross to Parkes was the match ball with which he scored one of his hat-tricks. No doubt it was partly Cross's way of expressing his relief that precious few of the keepers he faced were in Parkes' class.

CHAPTER 5

Alvin Martin

When Alvin Martin discusses the art of being a top-class defender, you are immediately reminded of Sherlock Holmes unravelling a murder mystery and telling his bemused sidekick: 'Elementary, my dear Watson.' Martin, arguably the best of all West Ham's post-war centre-halfs, says: 'Football's a simple game, but people do complicate it at times. The best way I can describe it is that there are a lot of simple little basic rules – things like not diving in for the ball unless you have a good chance of getting it and not messing about on the ball in areas where the opposition might score if you lose it – and it all boils down to picking the simple, basic thing to do from maybe five or six options.'

Martin's ability in that department, already outlined by Phil Parkes' assessment of him and Billy Bonds as the best central defensive pairing he ever worked with, can also be seen in his 20-year professional West Ham record of more than 600 first-team appearances (from 1976 to 1996); his 17 England caps; and the fact that he was filling the number 5 spot when the Hammers achieved their greatest league success.

Martin had more injury problems than most; in only a handful of his 19 seasons at Upton Park did he manage to play in most or all of their league matches. It was significant that the seasons in which he made the most appearances included the 1980–81 campaign, when the Hammers achieved that remarkable Second Division Championship triumph, and the

1985–86 season, when they finished in their highest-ever position – third – in the First Division. That season, the first time and only time that West Ham have ever truly appeared to have the potential to lift the Championship, Martin had Tony Gale as his partner at the heart of defence (in the absence of the injured Bonds), and had taken over from Bonds as the captain. The absence of Bonds might well have been looked upon as the engine being ripped out of the side. On Bonzo's influence on the team in 1980–81, Phil Parkes says: 'His leadership was something else. I'm not just talking about his style of play, but also his willingness to take on the responsibility of organising people. If anyone took it upon himself to make sure that players were in the right positions, were doing the right things for the team, it was him.'

But fortunately for West Ham, Martin, having learned much from Bonds, was no shrinking violet in that department either. So much so that those who had rubbed shoulders with him in his early days at West Ham would surely have marked him down as a classic example of a poacher turned gamekeeper. Certainly, when it came to players doing the 'right' things, the Alvin Martin of season 1976–77 – his first as a professional – was totally different to the Alvin Martin of the 1980s.

The Bootle-born Martin, who joined West Ham as an apprentice at 16 as a result of Everton – where he had been an associate schoolboy player – only offering him a contract as an amateur, was fascinating on the subject in the autobiography (*A 21-Year Stretch*) with which he marked his Hammers testimonial year in 1995. He recalled: 'After a couple of months, I began to realise that I had as much, if not more, ability than the other young lads.

'That first year, 1974–75, was in fact easier than I had anticipated. We had a good youth team, including Alan Curbishley, Paul Brush, Geoff Pike and Terry Hurlock and reached the FA Youth Cup final [against Ipswich]. The following year, I was introduced to the first team, and again had a very good season. Then in my third year with the Hammers, things began to go wrong. I suffered a low and this was entirely down to me.

'Because I was finding it easy football-wise, I started to take liberties, which you just can't afford to do in this game. Instead of keeping it simple, I started to attempt the more difficult things at the wrong times. My form suffered as a result, and at this stage, I knew that the reserve-team manager Bill Lansdowne wasn't a fan of mine. After one particular game at Tottenham we had some heated words and he was more or less ready to wash his hands of me. To be honest, I think we were both ready to throw in the towel. I suddenly felt a long way from home and but for the intervention of Ron Greenwood [who had signed him] I might well have gone home.

'At that time in my career, I have to admit that I was maybe a bit too arrogant and cocky, and some of the senior players weren't slow to pass by an opportunity to put me in my place. I remember one incident when I happened to nutmeg John McDowell [in a training match] and, being the brash Scouser that I was, made John aware of the fact. Only it wasn't John who I upset. For some reason, Bonzo took real exception to what I had done and followed me around for the next five minutes waiting to seize his chance to teach me a lesson. The moment inevitably came, and after feeling the full force of his challenge from behind, I didn't think I would get up again.

'I would beat two or three people and then lose the ball in a bad position. I was getting more and more frustrated with myself and the way I was playing. It became a mental crisis for me, and I was very fortunate I came through it. There were times when, just 18 years old, I did go into the office to see Mr Greenwood – as I always called him – and John [Lyall] and asked them if I could go home, but Mr Greenwood always always responded with an emphatic no.

'It wasn't only me who suffered. My messing about with the ball used to wind the coaches up something rotten. Ron Boyce, who bore the brunt of all this, is usually a mild-mannered man who loves to have a laugh and a joke with you, yet when he does get heated up, he really flies off the handle.

'I remember when we were on tour in Germany, I started to flick the ball up and do a few tricks. Eventually, I came unstuck a couple of times, and we went in at half-time two or three goals down. Boyce was in the dressing-room before me, and as I walked in and went across to the table to get a cup of tea, he suddenly pounced on me, grabbed me by the throat and pinned me against the wall. No one else in our dressing room could believe their eyes. I was already 6ft 2in by then and here was Ron – some five inches shorter than me – almost lifting me off the floor. He looked me square in the eyes, his face was crimson with rage, and it seemed like he was going to explode. He called me a few names, and then told me to sit down.

'Looking back, I used to push Ron right to the limit. We laugh about it now.'

So, too, does Bonds, especially when he looks back on Martin's contribution to West Ham's valiant bid to break the Liverpool–Everton stranglehold on the Championship in 1985–86. As Martin says: 'Tony Gale was a good foil for me, but if anybody could be said to have helped bring the best out of me, it was Billy. When I played alongside him [in 1980–81], I did not feel there was anyone in the country who could ever intimidate us. With Ray Stewart on the right, and Frank Lampard on the left, we had an exceptionally strong, dependable back four. Even though the team as a whole were not geared to stopping people a lot of the time, I thought we were a match for most sides.'

One of the reasons for that concerns what Martin describes as the team's 'honesty'; the willingness of every player to hold his hands up over his mistakes and shortcomings – to put himself under the microscope in front of anyone else. The fact that they were honest with themselves meant that they could also be totally honest with each other without it leading to friction and undermining the crucial sense of unity and camaraderie in the side.

'In any team, it's no good unless the players are honest with each other,' he says. 'Once you have that, then you know where you're all going. You know that there are going to be setbacks along the way, but that you're going to get over them.'

Bonds, he recalls, did much to develop this in the West Ham dressing-room – and Martin likes to think that he maintained it in their big push for the First Division title. He says: 'As a professional footballer, you are always setting yourself targets, such as getting into the first team, establishing yourself in the first team, then getting into the England team and so on.

'But when you become a captain, you start looking at what you can get out of the rest of your team – not just yourself – and how you can draw people together. When I was made captain, I started to think about the game more, in the sense of how to deal with other people.

'I already knew how to deal with myself. One of the things I was taught by my father, from a very early age, was not to blame other people when things were not going right. If West Ham suffered a heavy defeat, I would always start off by looking at where I had been to blame. Sometimes I wished I could have changed that, to take the pressure off myself, but that was the way I was and, as a captain, it was something that I tried to instil into all the players I was working with. If you have 11 people who are that self-critical, you have 11 people who want to win, and 11 people who want to respect each other and want to help each other.'

Martin, an assertive figure, felt so strongly about the importance of an 'open' West Ham dressing-room atmosphere that he could almost be said to have encouraged players to 'take a pop' at each other. One example of the advantages of this concerned a period in the 1985–86 season, when Tony Cottee – whose striking partnership with Frank McAvennie had been a major factor in the Hammers' success – appeared to stop working as hard as he had done previously. Of the two, Cottee, more of a goal-poacher, found it more difficult to involve himself in the defensive side of the game – but this counted for little when the subject came up for discussion at the team meeting Martin initiated.

'We were all totally honest with each other. People started pointing the finger at Tony [because of his apparent lack of commitment] and, to his credit, Tony took everything they said on board and the next game he was back working as hard as ever.

'This was one of the great things about that team. The spirit was magnificent, everyone knew their job and if they didn't do it, then they had the rest of the lads to answer to. The manager would have found it a lot harder to pull anyone into line than the players – it worked brilliantly.

'Some players don't like it, but it's how they respond to it that matters. I used to have a lot of stand-up rows with Billy [Bonds], and also Ray Stewart and Julian Dicks. It was hard for me to admit that they were right in the heat of a game, but once I had time to think about it, I never had any problems in going back to them and admitting they were right. As a captain, I obviously had to think about the different personalities and temperaments of players. For example, if someone had a pop at someone, and I felt there was a danger of it having a negative effect, the onus was on me to try and ease the situation. I would probably go and put an arm around the player's shoulder and say: "But he's right, though, isn't he? Why don't you respond to it?"

'I enjoyed this part of the job – it was great for me because, quite apart from my desire to be in a successful team, it was getting me ready for management.'

No less pertinent to West Ham were the experiences that had prepared Martin to become one of Britain's most impressive all-round centre-halfs. More skilful on the ball than many of his rivals in other teams, he clearly learned quickly from those brushes with his fellow players and coaches at the start of his Upton Park career.

He says: 'From the moment I joined West Ham at 16, they started to teach me things that I'd never even heard mentioned at Everton. They were all simple things, basic habits like that of playing the simple ball when it was on, and letting the ball run across your body instead of stopping it, as Trevor Brooking used to do. You know, Trevor used to do things that would enable him to beat opponents without even touching the ball. I remember the word "habit" used to crop up all the time there. You get good habits and you become a good player, it was as simple as that. I couldn't take it all in quickly enough – I was so enthusiastic that I used to go back [for extra training and coaching] in the afternoons. So, in terms of getting football knowledge at an early age, it was the right club for me to be at.

'Even during my sticky spell there, when I went home to my digs at night wanting to pack it in, I knew deep in my heart that this wasn't an option for me. Though I might have felt like taking the easy way out, I knew that I wasn't the sort of person to do that. I was stubborn and I had to be true to myself.'

As far as his development as a player was concerned, Martin started with more going for him than most. In addition to his ability on the ball, he says: 'The thing I was always confident about was my ability in the air. When I was at my peak, I didn't think there was anyone stronger than me in that area. Whether I was attacking the ball in our box or their box, I can probably count on the fingers of one hand the number of times I was "done" in vital situations. It was one of my biggest strengths from a very early age.

'If there is one thing that I used to feel uncomfortable about, it was playing against small, quick players. It wasn't a big problem – I was as fit as anyone at West Ham, apart from Bonzo, and could run all day – but if someone really got at me, one against one, my concentration had to be 100 per cent. I learned to cope with it a bit more as I got older; in my younger days, I was probably too eager to win the ball and tended to get too tight on people, which gave them the scope to spin into the channels either side of me.

'Problems like these are part of your development process. The more games you play, the more that people learn about your strengths and weaknesses and think up ways to make things difficult for you. I should imagine that once I started to get established in the side, and teams got to know more about me, they would be saying: "Don't put the ball into their box because he is good in the air. Let's get the ball in behind their full-backs and force him to go to the flanks – he doesn't like that." You have to learn to combat things like that. It's the same with midfielders and forwards. Alan Devonshire [West Ham's midfielder] was superb at going past opponents with the ball, but after a while people started to drop off him so he had to find another way of beating them. He started to pass the ball more, he'd run with it so far then knock it off and go again for the return. He just kept adding more strings to his bow.

'In my own case, the way West Ham played probably accentuated my problem. In my early days with the club, their approach to the game was based on creative skills. It was like: "Well, you attack us, and we'll attack you." I won't say that the defensive side of the game – the business of putting the opposition under pressure when they had the ball – was never addressed, but it certainly wasn't as big a priority as it is with most other teams. It made it hard for any West Ham back-four man because if people aren't being put under much pressure further up the field, they obviously have the scope to give their front men the service they need.

'This was one of the reasons why there was little point in West Ham using an offside trap [with the back four men holding their positions in line with each other across the field, and pushing forward as a unit to compress the play]. I remember we tried it in a pre-season match against Ajax, which wasn't exactly the best time to use a system like that in view of the quality of their players and the fact that you need all 11 players to be switched on to it, not just the goalkeeper and the back four. We lost 4–0 and immediately reverted to our usual way of playing. So for most of my time at West Ham our approach at the back was to go with runners [which meant having to follow an opposing striker into different areas, as opposed to staying in the middle and leaving it to someone already in that zone to deal with the player]. Bonzo and I would often find ourselves going with people into the wide positions, which made it quite hard physically as well.'

Among the other important elements in Martin's development process was his experience of playing for England. His West Ham performances in their 1980–81 Second Division Championship-winning season had led to Greenwood giving him his first cap against mighty Brazil and the likes of Socrates and Zico at Wembley in May 1981. Although England were beaten 1–0 that day, Martin was kept in the squad by his former

West Ham boss at least until the 1982 World Cup finals, when he was left out because of doubts about his fitness after injury, and by Greenwood's successor, Bobby Robson.

By the start of the 1985–86 season, his total of England appearances stood at 13 and he recalls: 'I was beginning to reap the benefit of working with Don Howe [the England assistant manager and a man noted as an outstanding coach of defensive techniques]. Thanks to Howe, I started to look at the defensive side of things more closely, and I thought about how I could take some of the things he said and incorporate them into my game as a West Ham player.

'For example, he used to talk a lot about the advantages of marking in front of players – the "wrong" side he called it. The old-style was marking goal-side, but teams had moved on – Liverpool, Arsenal and Everton had all started marking on the "wrong" side – and I quickly found that by doing this at West Ham we were able to give sides less scope to get the ball in the channels against us.'

On top of all this was the influence of John Lyall, who had installed Martin as a regular member of the West Ham side in 1979 and who was to prove rather more sympathetic to the problems of his defenders than Greenwood had been.

'John was less of a purist. He liked his team to play constructive attacking football, but he also liked his team to get stuck in and be organised. The training under John's management was always very difficult. I remember a number of players who joined West Ham then were expecting the training to be all nicey-nicey and were amazed at how hard it was. It was really driven home to me when I was with the England squad – I found the England training sessions a doddle compared to the work I had to do at West Ham. John wanted his players to be super-fit because he appreciated that the only time you can get consistently good results is to work hard off the ball to stop people creating chances against you. I would say that when he was manager, that aspect of the game at West Ham was possibly addressed more than ever before.

'Some of the players he brought in might not have been as

talented in the creative sense as your Trevor Brookings but they contributed a lot in other ways. There are times when your great ball-players are going to have an off-day, and that's when you need to be able to dig in and still get a result.'

All of which brings us back to those West Ham teams of 1980–81 and 1985–86. 'During my West Ham career, they were the periods when the club came closest to getting the balance right,' Martin says. The bottom line was that in both those seasons West Ham were boosted not just by their back four but by the willingness and ability of their colleagues to produce what Martin describes as a 'complete team performance'.

In the 1980–81 season, Martin and company – Stewart, Bonds and Frank Lampard – had been helped by the 'defending from the front' of Paul Goddard and David Cross. In 1985–86, when his back-four colleagues were Stewart, Gale and Steve Walford or George Parris, this vital element was provided by Cottee, who had been brought into the team three seasons earlier, and Frank McAvennie, who had been bought from St Mirren in the summer of 1985.

Martin recalls: 'Both players worked exceptionally hard, as did little Mark Ward [the winger who also joined the Hammers in the close-season from Oldham]. Phil Parkes was as solid as ever in goal, and we had Neil Orr or Geoff Pike just sitting in front of us and feeding the more creative midfielders, Alan Devonshire [back in action after a 19-month absence through injury] and Alan Dickens [Brooking's successor following the England star's retirement in 1983].'

As far as Cottee and McAvennie were concerned, Martin says: 'I would hate to have been playing against these two at that time. Both had tremendous pace and I lost count of the number of times that Tony Gale or I would hit a long ball over the top of the opposing defence and get them in with just the keeper to beat.' He is particularly enthusiastic about the difference McAvennie made, pointing out that expending bags of energy – off the ball as well as on it – came rather more naturally to him than it did to Cottee, and that being relatively unknown in English football, he was able to take opponents by surprise. He scored 26 league goals that season, six more than Cottee, but he also inspired the Hammers through his non-stop running, his passing and crossing and his tackling.

'There are a lot of things you can say about Frank McAvennie,' Martin says, referring to the headstrong, undisciplined streak he portrayed in his personal life – which brought him enough tabloid publicity to last a lifetime – and his laid-back approach on the training field.

'Frank was the worst trainer I have ever seen. But if he were at his peak today I dread to think what he would cost. You know, I have always felt that a team will never win the Championship with someone up front who is just a goal-poacher, a six-yard box player. No disrespect to people who have been in that category – the likes of Jimmy Greaves and Gary Lineker – but in my view it is absolutely essential to have strikers who can also contribute to a team in other ways. This is where Frank was so important to us. As an all-round forward, he was quite similar to Alan Shearer. Of all the strikers in the game that season, I would say that Frank was as close as anyone to being like Shearer is now.'

McAvennie, in fact, had joined West Ham as a midfield player, and for their first match of the season – a disappointing 1–0 defeat at Birmingham – he operated behind a front-line partnership comprising Cottee and Goddard. The latter had to be taken off with a damaged shoulder, which was to keep him out for virtually the rest of the season and which caused Lyall to view the Hammers' prospects somewhat pessimistically. 'I returned gloomily to London that evening,' he recalled. 'I realised that I had little option other than to change the formation and to play McAvennie as a striker alongside Cottee.' But this move, combined with that of bringing in Dickens to replace McAvennie in midfield, was to prove the making of West Ham as genuine title contenders. As Martin says: 'These enforced changes proved the final pieces of the jigsaw. Suddenly, we had a team in which all the players complemented each other.'

It took time for this to be translated into results – though the

Hammers beat QPR in their next match, this was followed by successive defeats against Luton and Manchester United. But from that point they established a club record of 18 consecutive matches unbeaten (a run that ended at Tottenham on Boxing Day) and finished the season with a total of 26 First Division wins, another club record. No less impressive was their solidarity at the back. They conceded just 40 goals, only three goals more than the Champions, Liverpool, and one goal fewer than the runners-up, Everton. It is not unreasonable to suggest that, but for the disruption to the fixtures caused by adverse weather, and the extra strain West Ham experienced in an FA Cup run that took them to the FA Cup sixth round, Liverpool and Everton would have had even greater cause to worry about their challenge. By the time the Hammers were knocked out of the Cup by Sheffield Wednesday in March, they were 10 points behind that awesome Anfield machine, but had four matches in hand. But they lost their next two league matches, to Arsenal and Aston Villa; and after regaining the winning habit against Wednesday, they were faced with the daunting prospect of having to play their 13 remaining matches in 37 days – and the last five of those games in ten days.

During that period Martin's leadership qualities were illustrated more vividly than ever. One game which he and his admirers could hardly forget was the one against Newcastle at Upton Park on 21 April, when the centre-half scored a hat-trick against three different keepers in an 8–1 win. The keepers he beat were Martin Thomas, who was in pain from the start because of a shoulder injury and eventually went off just after half-time; Newcastle's little Northern Ireland striker, Ian Stewart; and finally Peter Beardsley. Martin rated his goal against Beardsley, when he sent the England star the wrong way with a penalty, as the best of the three. Lyall, though, did not share his delight. 'He wasn't very happy that I had taken the kick,' Martin recalls. 'Ray Stewart was our regular penalty-taker, and John felt that because of our need to improve our goal difference, I should have insisted on his taking the kick.' However, there were no Lyall complaints about Martin's actions in the three Upton Park matches that followed – the drive and know-how that brought them nail-biting wins over Coventry (1–0), Manchester City (1–0) and Ipswich (2–1). Lyall himself has gone on record as saying that Martin's performance against Ipswich, when the Hammers had to come from behind for their victory (achieved, ironically, through a Stewart penalty), was one of his best for the club.

At that stage the Hammers were four points behind Liverpool with a game in hand. Liverpool's last game was against Chelsea at Stamford Bridge. On the same day, West Ham had to play at West Bromwich Albion, who had already been relegated, and finally at Everton (who were by then out of the title race) three days later. Sadly, though West Ham beat West Brom 3–2, Liverpool also collected maximum points to mark Kenny Dalgish's first season as their player-manager with a record 16th Championship triumph.

It was a remarkable season for Dalglish, whose team also beat Everton in the FA Cup final. Despite the fact that West Ham lost their chance of at least finishing in the First Division runners-up spot through going down 3–1 at Goodison, it was a remarkable season for them, too. The big question, of course, is why they were unable to build on it and keep going from strength to strength. Martin suggests it was partly due to the 'if-it-ain't-broke-don't-mend-it' philosophy. One example of how this rebounded on the Hammers was the case of Cottee and McAvennie, and the manner in which opposing sides made life more difficult for the pair the following season by leaving less space behind their back four. Thus Cottee and McAvennie, who had repeatedly been able to use their pace to get behind defences, were rendered less threatening. 'No matter how successful a team might have been, I think it is still important that they get in new players if only to increase competition for first-team places and stop people becoming complacent.'

There are other areas of regrets for Martin. When looking back on his England career, for example, he still believes that Robson made a mistake in the 1986 World Cup finals in Mexico by leaving him out of the side for the quarter-final against

Argentina – the Diego Maradona 'Hand of God' game – in favour of restoring Terry Fenwick to the line-up after injury. He had performed well in the previous match, the 3–0 win over Paraguay, and England's 2–1 defeat by Argentina virtually signalled the end of Martin's international career (he played his last England game against Sweden at the start of the following season). Still, while bemoaning that World Cup experience, he admits: 'I'm not sure I expressed myself enough as an England player. I went out determined not to let the team down, and just did a job, whereas at West Ham I went out to be the leader, to dominate whoever I was up against, to go forward with the ball and involve myself in the attacking picture, to help everyone around me . . . I don't know, as an England player, I just think I was too inhibited.'

What matters to him more than anything, though, is the way he is perceived by West Ham fans and those who played with him at Upton Park. The memories of Martin in that claret and light-blue jersey are nothing if not evocative, especially when he ended his career at Upton Park in the 1995–96 season by helping them recover from a bad Premiership start with four wins and five draws from the ten games in which he figured in their starting line-up. Not bad for an injury-ravaged 37-year-old who was playing on borrowed time. When it comes to going past your sell-by date, the big Scouser was in a class of his own – as Billy Bonds can confirm. One of Bonds' most remarkable decisions during his spell as West Ham's manager (February 1990 to August 1995) was to give Martin a new contract and bring him back into the side after having given him a free transfer. At the root of it all was the Achilles problems Martin was suffering. In December 1990 he was forced out of action for 16 months, and in February 1993 he was ruled out for ten months. To Martin, these problems were merely the end result of a much more agonising experience – that of serious trouble with the insteps of his feet, mainly caused by an arthritic condition which had necessitated three operations (two on the right, one on the left) and affected other parts of his body.

'I first started having problems with my right foot when I was

Ronnie Boyce gives new meaning to his reputation for playing with the head rather than the heart

OPPOSITE PAGE
TOP: John Lyall, a football romantic with a tough, pragmatic streak

BOTTOM: The crowning glory: the regal Bobby Moore shows England manager Alf Ramsey the World Cup after the epic victory over West Germany in 1966

THIS PAGE
TOP: Vintage Martin Peters, a player renowned for ghosting into scoring positions

RIGHT: A sight guaranteed to strike fear into the hearts of West Ham's opponents: Alan Devonshire running at them with the ball

ABOVE: Billy Bonds adds determination and physical power to West Ham's silky skills

TOP RIGHT: Trevor Brooking again comes top of the class in the creative midfield arts

RIGHT: The finishing touch: Geoff Hurst displays the commitment that helped make him the Alan Shearer of his day

Rio Ferdinand, the most exciting West Ham defender for years

Julian Dicks, 'the last real Upton Park hero left'

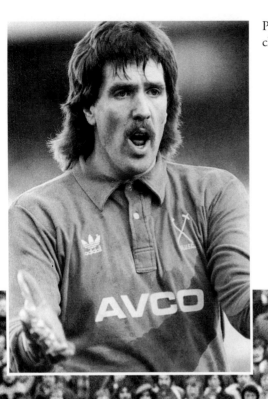

Phil Parkes, the holder of West Ham's clean-sheet record

Heading for the top, Alvin Martin style

a young lad at the club, after somebody had caught it with his boot as I was trying to clear the ball during a match against Wrexham. In retrospect, I know that I must have damaged a bone, but at the time I didn't bother to get it X-rayed – I was a young lad trying to stay in the team – and kept on playing. Six weeks later, it felt okay. But when I got to around 27 or 28, I started to get problems with it again and it just got increasingly worse.

'Once I got that foot sorted out, I experienced the same symptoms in the other. So then I thought: "What do I do?" I'd had a load of problems with the first operation, it had changed the whole mechanics of the foot. I had a big bunion on the side of my big toe that pushed my foot inwards and made me run over on one side of my foot, so they decided to remove another bone.

'But once you start messing around with your feet, it is an absolute nightmare, so when I started getting trouble with the left, the specialist advised me to keep on playing with it as long as I could. To be fair, that was the one bit of advice that I should not have taken – I should have said, "No, sort my feet out once and for all." It would not have mattered how long it would have taken, at least I would have had it behind me and could do myself justice as a player.

'As it was, I had maybe two years when West Ham's supporters must have thought I had gone. The people who watched me play at West Ham knew what level I could perform to, and the fact that I wasn't able to get to that level was very hard for me to take. Playing at 80 per cent might be okay for some players, but not for me. The fans expected me to be a leader, to be aggressive and to be skilful. They didn't expect me to just whack the ball into the stand.'

It was towards the end of the 1991–92 season, when Martin was on the way back to full fitness, that Bonds told him that the time was ripe for him to bring down the curtain on his Hammers career.

Martin recalls: 'Bill said, "I don't think you can do it any more." He was as honest as anyone has ever been with me. I thought: "Right, I've got eight weeks to get myself fully fit and strong and prove him wrong." I actually got myself match-fit in the reserves, at a time when they'd technically given me a free transfer, and Bill obviously knew I was back to normal and could do a job for him because he played me in the last seven matches of the season.'

Though Martin continued to be dogged by injuries, Bonds gave him one-year contracts throughout the rest of his time as manager, and his successor Harry Redknapp followed suit for the first season that he was in charge. When Martin did reach the end of the road at Upton Park, before the start of the 1996–97 season, he moved to Leyton Orient. Then it was on to his first managerial job, at Southend. As with Bonds, who joined Millwall as manager at roughly the same time, he deserved some sympathy. The standards he set himself at West Ham meant that he had a lot to live up to.

CHAPTER 6

Rio Ferdinand

To those who have been watching West Ham the longest, the obvious question to arise from a glance at this fantasy XI is: 'What is Rio Ferdinand doing in a team like this?'

Bobby Moore and Alvin Martin, his central defensive colleagues, were Hammers legends, two of the longest-serving and most accomplished players in the club's history. In contrast, Rio Ferdinand, just turned 19, has only recently come on to the first-team scene. He made his first appearance when coming on as a substitute for the last 20 minutes of the Hammers' final Premiership match of the 1995–96 season against Sheffield Wednesday and by the start of the 1997–98 season, he had barely 16 league games to his name.

But Ferdinand can hardly be described as just another youngster struggling to gain a foothold in the game. One reason why he has attracted more attention that most is that he is a cousin of the Tottenham and England centre-forward, Les Ferdinand. The other is that he is widely acknowledged to be the most talented young defender in Britain.

It says much about the potential he showed as a regular member of the England Youth team that Terry Venables brought him in to train with the senior squad in Euro 96, an arrangement that has continued under Glenn Hoddle. Like Venables, Hoddle believed that Ferdinand could only benefit by rubbing shoulders with the best. So just think about how far he could progress if he were to have a Bobby Moore and an Alvin Martin alongside him each week. Just think, too, about how those old masters would relish having an apprentice of Ferdinand's quality.

The game is littered with the sad stories of prodigies who have failed to keep their feet on the ground and faded into obscurity or blown up spectacularly before crossing the finishing line. The goldfish bowl that is professional football demands a level of maturity – a sense of independence and responsibility – that only a few youngsters are able to cope with. The more talented the youngster, the more pronounced this problem becomes, which helps explain why Manchester United's manager, Alex Ferguson, has been so conscious of the need to shield his own young stars like Paul Scholes and David Beckham from the hype that has accompanied their steps up the ladder.

There have already been signs of Ferdinand needing protection himself. His whole world seemed to collapse at the start of the 1997–98 season when he was poised to make his England début in the World Cup qualifying tie against Moldova at Wembley, only to rule himself out as a result of a drink-driving charge. In normal circumstances, England's coach Glenn Hoddle might well have been prepared to overlook this embarrassing episode. But it coincided with the death of Diana, Princess of Wales – and reports that the driver of the car involved in that fatal crash was over the drink-drive limit. Thus, in the circumstances, the usually tolerant Hoddle was forced to take the view that the inclusion of Ferdinand in his line-up would be improper and insensitive.

The extraordinary thing about this episode in the Ferdinand success story was that it was so unexpected. There had been nothing in his football background to suggest that he might falter in this way and, indeed, the general consensus of opinion was that this out-of-character problem for him would prove very much an isolated hiccup in his career.

For this reason alone, Moore and Martin would have no problems in relating to him. Martin, West Ham's centre-half when Ferdinand was coming up through the Upton Park schoolboy and youth ranks, found him the most receptive of pupils – a young man with an enquiring mind and the same gargantuan appetite for self-improvement that helped Martin reach the top. Moore, despite his image as an aloof, self-centred figure, would surely have warmed to this side of Ferdinand, too. Moore believed that each player should take responsibility for himself, his fitness and his actions, and responded best to those who felt the same way. In other words, most of his help was directed towards those who helped themselves.

The other factor which ties the three together is that the six foot two Ferdinand, like Moore and Martin, is what coaches describe as a 'ball-playing' central defender, a player who is sufficiently comfortable on the ball to be able to go forward with it or make a constructive pass to suddenly put the opposition on the back foot. As defenders, Moore and Martin leaned heavily on their anticipation. This particularly applied to Moore, whose ability to read the game enabled him to dispossess opponents almost before they realised what was happening. Time and again, Moore would see what was in the mind of the passer before he put foot to ball, and it was rare that he failed to win the ball cleanly and with the minimum degree of physical contact. Inevitably, Ferdinand has yet to reach that level of awareness, and it is possible that he never will for the simple reason that his need to do so is not as great as it was for Moore. He has greater pace than both the former England captain and Martin, and has the edge in terms of athleticism.

It could also be argued that he is the most versatile of the trio, having looked entirely comfortable not just as a central defender but also as a midfielder (the role in which he started his West Ham career) and even as a striker. The ability of players to fill different positions or roles, thus giving their team the opportunity to alter its tactics and the shape of the side during a match without any changes in personnel, has long been a feature of the leading Dutch teams. The most famous example is Ajax, whose approach to the development of young players – 'multi-purpose' players, as opposed to 'specialists' – has attracted the attention of managers and coaches throughout the world. Until recently, such players have been rare in English football, hence the view that English teams have been too stereotyped. Ferdinand is a member of a new breed who are beginning to change all of that.

The strange thing about it in his case is that Ferdinand, born and raised in Peckham, south London, might well have been viewed as having undergone a football-passion bypass operation when he was a boy. He did not *dislike* football, but at the same time he was not one of those kids who always had a ball under their arm wherever they went, or who drove neighbours crazy by repeatedly kicking the ball into their gardens. Ferdinand barely played football at all.

'To be honest, I only started thinking about football when I was about 11 or 12. Before then, I was into athletics and gymnastics. I mucked about a bit playing football at school or with my mates on the estate where I lived, but it was never serious. At no time did I want to become a footballer.

'Initially, the only reason I began to take more of an interest in the game was that my cousin, Benny, played for a Sunday League team which was being run by my uncle – it was called Bloomfields – and he kept telling me I should come along. "You're really quick – you would be really good," he'd say. The problem was that they trained on a Saturday, the day I was involved in gymnastics. But eventually I had a free weekend, went and trained with Bloomfield and, as I had nothing much else to do, I agreed to play for them the next day.'

Once Ferdinand had started the ball rolling as a member of the Bloomfields team, there was no stopping him. At that level, just his strength and balance – qualities honed by his involvement in gymnastics – were enough to cause him to stand out. His balance was outstanding for someone of his height. In addition to the advantages this gave him in the defensive sense in terms of his being able to make a difficult tackle without going to ground, it also provided the scope for him to play his way out of situations in which most other players would have been forced to boot the ball into the next field. So in no time at all Ferdinand started to attract the attention of the professionals. Within a month of his turning out for Bloomfields he was invited to attend Queen's Park Rangers' School of Excellence. 'I was there for about three years and that's when the football interest really took off for me.'

At a time when Ferdinand was starting to look at other career-start options, the next step for him came through his friendship with a West Ham scout by the name of Dave Goodwin, the manager of the local district secondary schoolboys' team in which Ferdinand had played. Ferdinand still looks upon Goodwin as one of the men who must take most of the credit for his early success in the game. 'Football-wise, I would say that my association with him was probably the best thing that ever happened to me. Ever since I first met him, he has taken me under his wing and given me good advice.' Goodwin, indeed, was virtually an extension of the Ferdinand family. He was also a friend of Frank Lampard Snr, West Ham's assistant manager. 'Dave kept telling Frank Lampard to come and look at me, and it was Frank who first asked me to come to West Ham,' says Ferdinand. 'By that time, there were a number of other clubs showing interest in me – including almost all the London clubs – and I wanted to have a look at all of them. But Frank just kept on at me.'

To a great extent, his decision to sign for the Hammers was one which was made with his heart rather than his head. They were not the club who presented the best chances of success, in terms of Championship and FA Cup medals, but few of the others Ferdinand visited could match their open, friendly atmosphere.

As Ferdinand confirms: 'I think I really decided to join West Ham because they were the club who made me feel the most wanted, and everybody made you feel so much at home. It helped that I knew a few of the players from when I was younger, and I was also impressed by their comments about their determination to give young players a first-team chance. But it was the family atmosphere at Upton Park that really swung it for me.'

One figure who can discuss Ferdinand's progress at West Ham with greater authority than most is Tony Carr, the Hammers' youth team coach. Carr, who once spent two years on the staff as a centre-forward before drifting into non-league football and finally calling it a day as a player as a result of a broken leg, has been involved in the development of a number of outstanding schoolboy and youth players since his return to the club in 1980. His most notable protégés have included Tony Cottee, Paul Ince and Alan Dickens – and he has no hesitation in adding Ferdinand to the list.

He says: 'Our main football philosophy here is "control and pass". I know there is more to the game than that, there is determination, aggression and all those sorts of things, but we do put a lot of emphasis on the technical side of the game and this is where Rio could be described as a typical West Ham player. I did not have a lot of work to do with Rio because as soon as he joined the club [at 14] it was obvious he had a lot of natural ability. What you try to do is knock off the rough edges, make them more tactically aware and knowledgeable about the game. But I can't pretend as a coach that I have added to Rio's technical game at all. I think he was always a very technical player.'

Ferdinand says: 'Tony is another person I owe a lot to. He will always tell you straight if you are not pulling your weight, or you are playing badly, no matter how good you are or how good other people think you are. He started coaching me when I was in my last school year, just before West Ham signed me as a YTS player. To be honest, I'm not sure that he really fancied me to begin with.'

But Carr certainly did on the night that Ferdinand produced what the player considers to be one of his best-ever performances for the club. It came in the second leg of the South-East Counties League Cup final against Chelsea, when Ferdinand – then 16 and still at school – lifted the Hammers' youth team to the most improbable of victories.

Carr says: 'That was the game where I looked at Rio and thought: "There is something special here." In normal circumstances, he would have been regarded as too young to be in that team and he didn't play in the first leg, which Chelsea won 5–2. For the second leg, I was without a couple of our senior players – they joined the first-team squad on a tour of Australia – so I had to put in some schoolboys to make up the numbers.'

The coach must have thought that his worst nightmares were about to become reality when Chelsea made it 6–2 on aggregate in the opening minute. But the Hammers fought back to make it 6–6, with Ferdinand scoring one of the goals and creating two others, and after extra time, they scraped through on penalties.

'We played Rio in midfield, in a free role just behind the forwards, and he just revelled in it,' Carr recalls. 'He was only a kid, and I thought: "Well, if he can play like this, in this sort of company, we've really got a footballer here." I know it sounds a bit dramatic, but that's exactly how I felt about Rio.'

For all his expertise in creating and scoring goals, it is at centre-back – where he can use his football intelligence, mobility and physical power to stop them – that Ferdinand is clearly going to be one of Europe's leading football lights. West Ham came to this conclusion in an end-of-season friendly against Charlton, when Ferdinand – still a schoolboy – was handed the number 5 jersey as a result of the players in contention for the job not turning up. 'They asked me if I liked playing there,' Ferdinand says, 'and I just said that as long as I was in a side, I didn't really mind where I was put. The next season I played there again in a reserve match against St Albans. Ever since then I have been seen primarily as a centre-back.'

More pertinent is that, with his skill and composure on the ball, he is seen as the ideal player to operate as one of three central defenders – a system that, with so many opposing teams using only one recognised central striker, gives men like him greater scope to occasionally break free of their defensive responsibilities and involve themselves in the play further forward. Ferdinand had plenty of practice in the 1995–96 season, in the vintage West Ham youth team which reached the final of the FA Youth Cup – beating Arsenal, Chelsea and Tottenham before losing to Liverpool – and won the South-East Counties League title.

Carr explains: 'We decided to play three at the back. It worked well because Rio was so comfortable coming out with the ball. He could break into midfield and give us more control of the game. We spoke to Harry [Redknapp] and he felt that it was worth giving it a try in the first team as well as in the youth side. He said: "Let's try and play that way throughout the club." We felt it was the way forward in England, especially with so many foreign players coming into the game. There was a lot more emphasis on teams keeping possession and playing out from the back, rather than just hitting it straight into the front players.'

Ferdinand had clearly enjoyed himself in that youth team, and not just because of his and their success. As he says, it was a team in which everybody was equal and everybody had a share of control.

'There was a fantastic atmosphere in the squad. We really enjoyed training, we had some really good laughs, and it helped us to become better players and be closer to each other. Of course, we had the odd argument and fight but then so does everybody. We used to go out together socially, whereas the people in the team the year before tended to go off and do their own thing. If you have a team that gels off the pitch, it has more chance of gelling on it. If your mate is getting slaughtered at left-back, you will go across and help him. Some were better than others but nobody would ever say that. It didn't matter who you were, you had to pull your weight. If you didn't, then anybody had the right to tell you to do it. You accepted it.'

It was about time that West Ham received some credit for their youth system, especially in view of the publicity directed towards the high-priced foreign players Redknapp was bringing to the club. Unfortunately, for all the expertise and hard work of men like Carr (who has played a major part in revamping and improving this aspect of the Hammers' set-up) the standard of the crop of youngsters coming into the club as schoolboys can vary from year to year.

'I do think there was a batch of players who came together in that 1995–96 team – Ferdinand, Frank Lampard Jnr, Lee Hodges and Manny Omoyinmi – who made all the difference. They were basically the backbone of the team. We did not have those four players the following season and, although we did quite well, we never hit the same heights.'

Still, the youth team's loss was very much the first-team's gain. Even at 17, the age when he stepped on to the big stage for the first time against Sheffield Wednesday, it did not take Ferdinand long to acclimatise himself to the game at this level. Remembering his feelings when called off the substitutes' bench, he says: 'When Frank [Lampard] said go and warm up, I was crapping myself. Then I heard the crowd behind me shouting "Rio, Rio – go on, son, get on." I looked up and saw Harry waving at me. The first time I touched the ball it went into Row Z. The crowd went crazy, they started laughing. But from that moment I was relaxed – I wasn't nervous at all.'

It was a similar story soon afterwards when Terry Venables asked him to take part in training with the England Euro 96 squad. This was a different league altogether, and not just in terms of skill and experience. How would these people, these superstars, take to a kid who was getting special treatment and who was gatecrashing their party? He was happy and safe in the warmth of the youth team, where everybody cared for everybody else, but he barely knew these people.

Ferdinand needn't have worried. He recalls: 'When I first arrived there [at England's training headquarters] I was in absolute awe. But once I got on to the training ground I just blanked out everything and concentrated on what I was doing. Everybody made me feel part of the squad, part of England. Ian Wright was really good, he would talk to you and encourage you, and of course Les my cousin, too. It was hard to believe but they made me feel like an England player, not just somebody who was making the numbers up in the training sessions.'

Glenn Hoddle, Venables' successor, moved him closer towards an England cap when he brought him into the squad for the World Cup qualifying tie against Italy at Wembley the following season. 'He said that he'd included me as part of the squad but to keep the pressure off me he would put me down as part of the get-together for training purposes,' Ferdinand reveals. Needless to say, Hoddle was anxious to keep the spotlight off Ferdinand for as long as possible. The same applied to his assistant, John Gorman.

'My first assignment after Euro 96 was to go up to Lilleshall and watch the England Under-18 players training. Of course, Rio was in that squad and did look a bit of a good prospect,' recalls Gorman. 'What immediately impressed me about him was the confidence in his own ability. It's nice to see somebody who has that kind of belief, particularly when it is a defender who likes to play out from the back. He is not frightened, he is very cool on the ball.

'He has shown up very well at senior squad training sessions, too. The biggest compliment I can pay him is that he never looked out of his depth. He was there to make up the numbers, give us some extra bodies in training. But that is what we do with the youngsters, to see how well they handle the situation. He handled it very well. I don't want to go overboard on Ferdinand, it's still very early stages. It's not fair on the boy if we do that. At the present time, though, we are very happy with his progress and Harry Redknapp and his staff should be complimented. It's nice to know there is the possibility of a ball-playing defender coming through because that fits in with the way Glenn and myself want England to play.'

The pace at which the different strands of Ferdinand the footballer have all come together is remarkable. A number of people have contributed to what he is today. But so, too, has Ferdinand, not just in the way he has performed on the pitch but also in the manner in which he approaches life. He seemed little short of devastated by his drink-driving incident before the Moldova game, and those close to him insist that if anyone is going to learn from an experience like that, it is Ferdinand. Certainly, it is easy to forget how quickly he has come to the fore and that like any young man of his age, it is unreasonable to expect a totally blemish-free development process. 'When I turned professional I knew it was only the start,' he says. 'I never once felt that was it, the end, and I could sit back and expect an easier life. West Ham wouldn't let me do that in any case. They get on to you even more when you turn professional.'

Carr says of him: 'He always has a smile on his face. He is a very jovial character but in the right way. He takes his game very seriously. I have never had a cross word with him, not really. He is a very deep-thinking player and will add his own bit to it. He will ask about this and about that but he thinks for himself, too. For a young player he has good knowledge.

'He gets very annoyed when he has played badly or made a mistake. He can get very upset when the team have lost, and that's a good sign because it shows how much he cares about the game.

'We know he is comfortable in the England environment. We get feedback, Harry gets feedback. Mentally, Rio is very strong. He would come back from those England get-togethers and I would ask, "How did you do?" He would say things like: "You should have seen how so-and-so did this, it was terrific." He is particularly enthusiastic about working with Alan Shearer.

'He acts like you would expect a youngster to act – he gets all excited. But you know that when he was there he wasn't overawed. He would show a tough edge to his character.'

It is one tough enough to suggest that even being alongside Bobby Moore and Alvin Martin, not to mention all the other distinguished members of a West Ham dream team, would not faze him either.

CHAPTER 7

Julian Dicks

At some time in its history, every club has a footballer who is elevated above all others by the fans, the media and even his own team-mates. Whether it is because of his ability or his behaviour – or both – his status verges on the iconic.

Two examples are Eric Cantona and Ian Wright, headstrong, individualistic figures who have repeatedly come into conflict with those who have sought to curb the demons in them. When Cantona and Wright have been punished for their mis-demeanours, the reaction from supporters has been so strong it is as if they themselves have been punished. After his suspension for attacking a Crystal Palace fan, Cantona was welcomed back by Manchester United supporters as an all-conquering hero, rather than as one who had brought shame on the club and the game itself. Despite Wright's countless bookings, dismissals, suspensions and fines, one would have to look long and hard to find any Arsenal fan who would not go into mourning if he were to leave the club. In terms of their popularity, their willingness to defy authority is as big a factor as their ability. We admire them because they touch the rebellious streak that lies in all of us. We want to be like them. We want to tell the boss where to go. We want to care a lot less about the repercussions of our actions.

All of which brings us to Julian Dicks, the number one Upton Park cult figure of the modern era – and the player who has to fill the left wing-back spot in any West Ham dream team. His recollection of a clash with Billy Bonds, when Bonds was his West Ham manager, says it all.

'There was one incident at Coventry. I elbowed Flynn, I think, or whatever his name was. I came in at half-time and Bonds has had a right pop at me. The kid had been on my back, so I'd given him a little elbow to dislodge him and get him off me. I hadn't caught him or anything, but he has gone down like a sack of shit. We've come in at half-time and Bill's come at me, ranting and raving. He said: "I should take you off." So I have taken my shirt off and thrown it at him and said, "Take me off then." He wanted to fight me. He said, "I will see you in the gym on Monday." I said: "Well, see me now. If you want to have a row, we'll have a row now."

'All the other players sat there in total silence with their arms by their sides and their heads bowed. Harry Redknapp [then Bonds' assistant] was saying, "Calm down, calm down," and, to be fair, he would have taken me off. But Bill said: "Get your shirt on, you're going out for the second half."'

That was not a difficult decision for Bonds because in many ways Dicks reminded him of himself. Bonds, a man who set a great store by professional discipline and propriety, would have hated to be described as 'The Terminator' – the tag attached to Dicks as a result of some of his most scary X-certificate tackles – but like Bonds, Dicks has played for West Ham as if his very life depended on their getting a result. Like Bonds, Dicks has been among the few West Ham players who have been capable of giving the team the edge over opponents in physical aggression and combativeness. And like Bonds, Dicks – probably the more skilful of the two – has provoked much amazement over the fact that he has been denied a place in the England team.

In truth, Bonds, and other managers who have worked with Dicks, have attracted some sympathy. It would have taken the patience of Job to turn a blind eye to the nightmare that Dicks inflicted upon himself in the 1992–93 promotion-winning season, when he was sent off three times – a hat-trick that no other West Ham player has experienced – and missed 13 games because of suspension. Nonetheless, Alvin Martin has said that if he had to select a team that had to win to save his life, Dicks would be the first man he would choose. The club's fanzine, *Over Land and Sea*, put it another way: 'Julian Dicks is the last real Upton Park hero left.'

Hence the disappointment among West Ham's fans when Billy Bonds sold Dicks to Liverpool in September 1993, as part of an exchange deal in which the lowly Hammers took David Burrows and Mike Marsh; and then their elation when Harry Redknapp (Bonds' successor) brought him back. Sometimes, a player is only fully appreciated when he is no longer there, and in this particular instance there is little doubt that West Ham's fans have grown even fonder of Dicks since his return. Those supporters were welcoming back a player who reflected their passion, their toughness – and their belief that West Ham should not allow themselves to be intimidated by anybody. For far too long, West Ham had a reputation for playing beautiful football but collapsing like a house of cards the moment the going got tough. The Hammers did start to become more resilient under the management of John Lyall (who signed Dicks from Birmingham for £300,000 in March 1988), but there have still been lengthy periods when Dicks has appeared to be ploughing a lone furrow, when a purist like Greenwood might well have viewed him as standing out at Upton Park like a sore thumb.

Dicks reacts indignantly to the view that the fouls which have led him into so much trouble with referees have been pre-meditated. 'I never tried to hurt anyone. No. In the tackle, yeah, but I have never gone in with the intention of breaking some-body's leg or anything. I wanted them to know I was on the pitch, yeah. But I would never set out to put them out of the match. I always, no mistake, went in for the ball. Nothing else. But if I hurt him, I hurt him, it wouldn't bother me.'

This is endorsed by a number of the players who have worked with him. For example, when Dicks was once sent off in a match against Arsenal for a second bookable offence (a late challenge on Ian Wright), the men who leapt to his defence included

Arsenal goalkeeper David Seaman. He had played with Dicks at Birmingham, and he said: 'He is a hard tackler and if it is not timed right it can look spectacular. But he is not a dirty player – he is not the type to cynically go over the top.' According to Dicks, winning the ball is 'as thrilling as scoring a goal'. He adds: 'I get a real buzz from winning a tackle, beating someone, there's nothing like it.' All defenders might say that, but it is doubtful they get the same high from it that Dicks experiences. He attaches considerable importance to gaining a psychological advantage over an opponent, dispossessing him powerfully enough to make him wary about crossing swords with the full-back again. Winning a tackle for him is taking a scalp. The bigger the name of the victim, the bigger the scalp. Maybe that explains why Dicks has an avid interest in the native American Indians. When Apache Indians take the life of a fellow warrior in battle, they take his power as well. To Dicks, it is the same when he comes away from a tackle with the ball.

The warrior in Dicks stems partly from his background. Recalling his upbringing in Bristol, he has said: 'Kids of seven and eight used to wander the streets after midnight. They would be glue-sniffing, breaking windows and stealing. The woman next door used to lock her kids out in the garden at night just to get some peace. I used to get into a lot of fights. All the usual reasons that kids fight. We'd be having a kick about, I would score and some kid would say it wasn't a goal, and the next thing we would be throwing punches. I never backed down and I could handle myself.'

His father, Ron, was a semi-professional footballer. He was a right-back and a tough tackler. Dicks couldn't show any signs of weakness. Ron had encouraged his son to be tough, to be a battler, to hate losing. A high pain threshold was integral to that image, which might go some way towards explaining why Dicks is noted as one of the top professional footballers who make the least fuss over injuries. In addition to his father, he was also influenced by his brother, Grantly. He was also a footballer, a semi-professional, a left-back – a hard tackler and a battler.

'Me and Grantly would be walking along and suddenly he

would slap me or trip me up and we would finish rolling around on the pavement. We were always fighting and arguing about something. We are close, we always have been, but that didn't stop us. We never stopped. Once when I was ten, he wound me up so much I grabbed a knife from the kitchen and chased him around the lounge with it. I just lost my rag with him. We laughed about it afterwards.'

The natural rivalry between siblings spilled over into football. It had to, as it was their father's passion, the thing he wanted his boys to excel at. It was how they could really impress him and win his affection and attention. So playing football was always going to be more intense than it should have been, to the point where there had to be a clear winner and loser, even if it meant the loser going home injured. 'Me and Grantly used to play a game, like a gunfight really, where we would stand ten yards apart, stick the ball in the middle, shout "Go" and charge. We used to go in as hard as we could, no matter how much it hurt, just clatter into each other to see who could come away with the ball. We would be at it for hours. It toughened up our tackling anyway.' Watch Dicks after he has clattered somebody to the ground. Seldom does he walk away and get clear of the scene. He is more liable to berate his victim for folding so easily, for being weak. He wants to rub salt in the wound, make sure the opponent knows it was him who had done the damage.

When he became an apprentice at Birmingham, he had to go on being tough. He was a boy in a man's world away from his home. He broke into the first team at 16. After 44 league games and one sending-off, he was being described by John Bond, his manager, as being 'skilful as well as hard as nails'. John Lyall echoed this view of Dicks when he brought him to West Ham. Nevertheless, that 'hard as nails' side of Dicks was difficult for West Ham to accept. True, they had other players who could put themselves about, but not to the extent that Dicks did. The so-called West Ham football 'Academy' – where everybody was supposed to be a gentleman – had landed itself with a full-back who had come to win at any cost and in his own way. They had got themselves a maverick – but the crowd loved him because he cared. If he sent somebody crashing into the advertising boards, was booked or sent off, he was forgiven because it showed he had as much passion for his team as those who paid to watch them.

Dicks didn't fall out with Lyall; there wasn't any time. There was always a battle to be fought against relegation, and Lyall was grateful to have a player who was so committed to the cause. West Ham could live with the maverick for a while. They had to.

When West Ham were finally relegated in 1990, the board did something that was against all its instincts – it replaced Lyall with an outsider, Lou Macari. This manager wanted discipline, more attention to pre-match preparations, more running in training, more long balls, and definitely no more room for those gentlemen who didn't mind too much if they lost, provided they did so playing that pretty football. It was time for the rod of iron. In one way, Dicks was exactly what Macari wanted: a fighter, a battler, a winner. But Dicks wouldn't fall in and salute. He trained the way he wanted to. He drank two cans of Coke just before a match and played short passes when Macari wanted long ones. The new manager was into authority and when a maverick gets the whiff of authority he does everything to defy it.

It didn't exactly help when, in the first encounter with Macari, Dicks was called a 'fat bastard'. That remark was the beginning of Macari's attempts to straighten the boy out. But Dicks was not for turning, he was going to go on doing it his way, even if that meant more bookings, dismissals and suspensions. He was going to show he was tougher than anybody else.

The relationship between Dicks and Macari's successor, Bonds, was not altogether harmonious either – especially when it came to training. Dicks trained as hard as the next man with the ball but cared little for the running Bonds used to thrive on. Both on and off the field, Dicks insisted on being Dicks, and following another sending off, Bonds decided that the time was right to let him go.

No doubt one of the big attractions for him in joining

Liverpool concerned the perception of their manager, Graeme Souness, as a kindred spirit. Ironically, Dicks was only booked once, which he himself felt was due to referees giving Liverpool players more 'benefit of the doubt'. But some members of the coaching staff were less enamoured with him than Souness was, and when Souness was forced to resign, Dicks – part of the manager's failed attempts to change the Bill Shankly culture that the club had once thrived on – soon found himself going through the Anfield exit door, too. A club that grew into a dynasty with the team ethic central to everything was no place for a maverick.

Dicks says: 'What I used to do, even at West Ham, was get a ball, go out half an hour before training, and smash it around. I've always done that. But at Liverpool they wouldn't let me do it. So I used to tell them to eff-off, go and get a ball and do it anyway. I had my fair share of arguments with Roy Evans and Ronnie Moran. Moran was the worst one – that's the one who wanted me out, Ronnie Moran. Those two are from the Shankly days. They still follow his methods today, which is fair enough. But if Souness had still been at Liverpool, I would still be there now.'

West Ham got him back at a perfect time, however. Something had happened to Dicks in Liverpool. He had matured. He had only been away for a year, but Peter Storrie, West Ham's managing director, has observed: 'You would not have recognised him as the same person.' Since then, Dicks has continued to have his brushes with referees from time to time, but most of the attention he has created has been focused on his considerable ability.

Dicks is very much a modern-day footballer. While full-backs have been encouraged to go forward for decades now, men like Dicks – wing-backs rather than full-backs – have added a new dimension to this aspect of the job. Dicks has always said that his first instinct is to attack and even in the days of the standard 4-4-2 formation, he regularly marauded upfield. In effect, he was ahead of his time – the time when teams would switch to 3-5-2, thus making attacking full-backs a vital component in that formation.

The only other recent West Ham left-back who could be favourably compared with Dicks is Frank Lampard, currently the club's assistant manager, who played for the Hammers from 1967 to 1985 and made 660 first-team appearances. His was a career packed with great moments. Who can ever forget the decisive goal Lampard scored – and that celebratory dance around the corner flag – in West Ham's epic FA Cup semi-final win over Everton in 1980? In addition to his West Ham honours, he also gained three England caps. Little wonder that Lyall described him as 'a very special player', adding: 'He was totally dedicated to his career, from the moment he came to me as a 15-year-old. He became a manager's dream. He was a prodigious trainer. When most of the players would be walking in for a shower after training, he would be lying on his back doing exercises. He was a player who thought about the game. Whichever player he marked, he made sure he knew about their strengths and weaknesses.

'Whenever I dropped him, he would never complain. He would listen to what you had to say and would then train by himself every afternoon until he got back in the side. Whenever I left him out, his response was "Okay, John, I'll be back".'

But for all that, how many West Ham fans would select Frank Lampard for a dream team place above Julian Dicks?

One of the many things Dicks has going for him is that he is a naturally left-sided player. Such players, like left-handed people, are thin on the ground, as reflected by the number of right-footed players who operate on the other flank. Having a left-footer of Dicks' quality is a bonus. Very few wide defenders can attack in the way Dicks does. Quite apart from doing all the routine work required of his type of player – such as moving forward to help out an attack that has stalled – he is an exceptionally dominating, assertive figure. While others see themselves as a supplement to an attack, he sees himself as the focal point of it. When he arrives on the outskirts of the penalty area he isn't there to play a minor role, as a bit-part player to keep everything ticking over before moving aside for a forward or midfielder. No, Dicks is there because he wants to be at the centre of it all.

He injects pace into an attack. He dribbles. He passes. He shoots. He is as comfortable in possession as any midfield ball-player. Back in 1987, the aspect of his game that most attracted John Lyall to him was his passing range. The kid could pass accurately both short and long. So many professionals are content just to make short, safe passes over five to ten yards. Dicks, though, can play the 'killer' ball.

Another Dicks speciality is changing the whole angle of an attack with a diagonal driven pass across the pitch. It is difficult to think of a midfield player who can execute this sort of move accurately, never mind a defender. David Beckham, the Manchester United and England midfielder, is the only other English footballer who regularly attempts it. The longer a pass has to be hit the easier it is to misjudge, particularly when it has to be struck through 45 degrees. Astonishingly, Dicks is accurate nine times out of ten. Such is his confidence in this department that on one occasion he staggered his colleagues by catching the ball on his right knee and, denied the time to allow it to drop, hit a left-foot volley straight to his target on the other side of the pitch.

But it is shooting ability that concerns opposing defences the most. As with Ray Stewart, the former West Ham right-back who took a total of 86 penalties but missed no more than ten, Dicks puts the emphasis on power in his own attempts to score from the spot. When he strikes the ball how he wants to strike it, the only way the keeper can stop it is if the ball hits him by accident. But no keeper would relish that – according to BSkyB, the Dicks penalty that enabled the Hammers to level the score at 2–2 against Manchester United in December 1996 travelled at over 90mph.

In open play, too, Dicks has never had to be encouraged to make a scoring attempt. Ian Bishop, the West Ham midfielder who was signed from Manchester City in 1989, recalls: 'In my early days at the club, I used to wonder why, when the players emerged from the dressing-room to begin training, Les Sealey [the keeper] was so grumpy. I eventually found out that, for an hour before, Dicks had been practising his shooting against him.' His shooting forms part of an attacking range that is a unique mixture of technique and power. His first goal for West Ham contained all those elements. It was against Arsenal at Highbury, on 4 Februay 1989. Dicks chested down a throw-in, burst past Lee Dixon and Steve Bould and rifled the ball into the roof of the net.

Perhaps one of the biggest compliments ever paid to Dicks came from Jim Smith, when he was manager of Portsmouth. 'You have to put someone on Dicks,' Smith declared. 'The fact that he is a left-back is misleading – the lad is so talented that he is quite capable of dominating the game from that position.'

In view of all this, it seems incongruous that Dicks, while being called up for the England B squad when Graham Taylor was manager, has never been given the chance to show what he can do in the full international set-up.

In the 1995–96 season, when the then Blackburn left-back Graeme Le Saux suffered a long-term injury before Euro 96, the door seemed wide open for Dicks to replace him. Instead, Terry Venables plumped for Stuart Pearce as his first choice, and Dicks was not even pushed into the squad as cover for him. It was against this background that Dicks became involved in a bizarre public clash with the England hierarchy over his shaven hair-style. Ted Buxton, Venables' chief scout, reportedly told Dicks' West Ham colleague, Slaven Bilic: 'He [Dicks] would have a better chance of making the England squad if he had a better haircut.' Buxton might well have had his tongue in his cheek – but Dicks, still nothing if not a non-conformist, clearly did not see the funny side of it. Tell Dicks to do something and he will do the opposite. In this instance, he hardly helped ease the situation with his newspaper outburst against the remark. If that's how they picked the England team, then he didn't want to know. But he had stood by his guns like he always does; and his fans were left to reflect on the possibility that maybe he was too much of a maverick to have been able to fit into the England set-up anyway.

In a sense, though Dicks was producing the best form of his career at the time – without being booked or sent off every other week – his omission from the Euro 96 scene did make some sense tactically. During Euro 96, Venables used two forwards, Darren Anderton and Steve McManaman, as wing-backs, rather than two defenders who played regularly as wing-backs for their club sides. Pearce was deployed predominantly as one of the three central defenders. Strange as it might seem, the role Pearce filled is the one that Dicks favours. He suggests that he is too attack-minded as a wing-back and is not somebody who can 'go up and down' in the way a wing-back should. Perhaps he was admitting that he would rather not have the responsibility of having to get back so quickly after getting upfield. If he were one of the three central defenders and went forward, there would still be plenty of cover, whereas a wide man has to guard his area of the pitch more carefully because so many counter-attacks start in wide positions. Unfortunately for him, appearing for England means doing exactly as the coach tells you. While Dicks' West Ham team-mates will compensate for the way he plays, England won't.

There was seemingly another opportunity for him to gain England recognition after Euro 96, when Pearce announced his retirement from international football and Le Saux was still injured – but Pearce was coaxed out of retirement by Glenn Hoddle, which sent the message that Hoddle didn't think anybody could replace Pearce or keep the position warm until Le Saux recovered. Then when the subject of how Dicks' image was being undermined by that haircut was raised publicly again, this time by Hoddle's assistant, John Gorman, the player sent a message of his own. He vowed that if ever England wanted him, he would turn them down.

He has since had other things to occupy his mind, not the least of these being the knee operation that caused him to miss the tail-end of the 1996–97 season and the opening months of the 1997–98 campaign. The question of whether this is liable to have any effect on his career at the top is a sensitive one for Dicks because he can claim to be fortunate to have lasted as long as he has following the left-knee cruciate damage he suffered in October 1990 which put him out of action for some 14 months.

The latest setback has come at a time when the Hammers have changed their style of play and do not need his determination and aggression as much as they have done in previous years. Following the disappointing performances of a number of Redknapp's foreign signings – at one time, the Hammers had more overseas players on their books than almost any other side in England – the club appear to have put a greater emphasis on British players. Among the most notable examples in the 1996–97 season were Steve Lomas, a tigerish, industrious midfielder, and John Hartson, a Joe Jordan-type centre-forward. The bottom line was that West Ham became more physical than they used to be.

Thus, just at the point Dicks has calmied down, the team could be said to be going in the opposite direction – the very direction which, in the past, caused Dicks so much trouble. The obvious advantage of this for someone like Dicks is that, with others sharing the battling load, he can concentrate more on expressing his skills; however, if this is the case, it will be because he wants it to happen. Though being himself has brought him a lot of criticism, it has also brought him affection and respect. For him, that will always far outweigh anything else.

CHAPTER 8

Trevor Brooking and Alan Devonshire

Successful teams, according to the former Southampton manager, Lawrie McMenemy, are all about a blend of men who can 'carry the piano, tune it and play it'.

It has been argued that, under the management of Ron Greenwood, West Ham placed too much emphasis on players in the latter category. It was both their strength and their weakness, and Greenwood himself was refreshingly honest about it. He said once: 'I accept much of the blame for this myself [West Ham's failure to land the Championship]. Perhaps I was too idealistic. Certainly, I was not ruthless enough. My conscience sometimes got in the way, and loyalty was occasionally a handicap. But I was not a dreamer. I believed in our style and was quite convinced that it was the best and right way to play. I honestly thought it could win the Championship for us. At the same time, I also recognised that it would be necessary for us to sweat and battle and, over the years, this was what let us down.'

Even so, when the men at the keyboard could come up with the tunes that Trevor Brooking and Alan Devonshire played in midfield, most people were too busy singing and dancing to worry overly much about it.

The great thing was how long the knees-up lasted. Brooking, born in Barking, east London, on 2 October 1948, was a first-team player at Upton Park from 1967 to 1984 and made a total of 635 appearances for the club. Devonshire, born at Park Royal, west London, on 13 April 1946, was on the playing staff from 1976 to 1990, and his number of first-team games was 446. So, in terms of their duets, the Brooking–Devonshire show at Upton Park ran for eight seasons.

The pair also played for England, of course – Brooking on 47 occasions, Devonshire on eight – but the only occasion they were in the same side was against Northern Ireland in 1980. At this level, Brooking found another player on his wavelength in the shape of Kevin Keegan. One of their best moments together was when England (then under Ron Greenwood's management) beat Italy 2–0 at Wembley in 1977 in a brave but vain bid to qualify for the 1978 World Cup finals. Brooking produced an outstanding pass to set up Keegan for the first goal. 'He directed it into an area that made me go forward and made me score,' Keegan recalled. It was Keegan who set up the second goal for Brooking, his first for England in 20 appearances. Brooking described his strike – with his left foot from just inside the box – as the 'finest shot of my career'.

Many believe that had Brooking and Keegan been in England's starting line-up for the 1982 World Cup tie against Spain in Madrid, England would have reached the semi-final. The pair, who had been out of action through injury, were only brought into the action by Greenwood for the last 20 minutes, with England needing a win to progress to the next stage. Despite the shortage of time left for him to adjust to the pace of the game, Brooking almost broke the deadlock with a shot which was foiled by Spain's keeper, Luis Arconada. But Keegan then missed a sitter – and England were out. So, too, were Brooking and Keegan; that defeat marked the end of their international careers.

Still, Brooking at least had the consolation of being able to revert to a similarly vibrant duet partner at club level.

While Brooking and Devonshire were no slouches as soloists, they were never more potent as creative forces than when they were together. Indeed, when discussing these players it is difficult not to talk about them as a pair, just as it is difficult to avoid talking about Bobby Moore, Martin Peters and Geoff Hurst as a trio. It is in midfield that a team's approach to the game is shaped, and if one believes in the principle that the pattern should start from keeping possession of the ball and creating chances, the argument for the presence of Brooking and Devonshire together in the West Ham dream team is simply overwhelming. This is particularly true with men like Billy Bonds and Julian Dicks ready to move up with them along the flanks and, when necessary, sort out any opponents who might take liberties with our outrageously talented duo (always assuming, of course, that any would-be football assassins could get close enough to them).

Brooking, who still turns out for a local amateur team at the age of 48, could have done with Bonds or Dicks when he was in Tbilisi for the Georgia–England World Cup qualifying tie in September 1996. In his capacity as a BBC TV match analyst, he took part in a so-called friendly match between the English and Georgian media representatives, with another footballing gentleman, BSkyB's Ray Wilkins, as one of his team-mates. During the game, an opponent brought him down with a two-footed tackle. As if this was not hard enough to take, another Georgian media man, clearly desperate not to miss out on the pleasure of cutting a big name down to size, hit the old maestro as he got up.

Brooking needed four stitches for a cut above the right eye, but it was typical of him that he should laugh off the incident. 'All through my career I had Bonzo [Bonds] looking after me,' he said. 'Now, at the first sign of trouble, who is there? Ray Wilkins!'

At least Brooking, 6ft tall and 12st 8lb, was well-made physically. Devonshire, 5ft 11in and 11st, looked frail in comparison, particularly at the start of his West Ham career when he had yet to develop the necessary muscle power to be able to fully capitalise on his ball skills. His image then as a player who might be blown over by a puff of wind was not improved when, on his first day of full-time training, he collapsed in a heap while running around the pitch and was off sick for ten days with a virus.

Not that being clogged had much effect on Dev and his West Ham midfield partner. They might not have had the combative streak of other midfield players but, more importantly, they had immense strength of character. Both men were masters of the main creative arts. Tackling was a bit of a problem for them (though they did try), and neither would cause any anxiety among opponents when the ball was in the air – good headers of a ball they certainly were not. But when they had the ball on the ground, their ability in passing it or running with it was a joy to behold. Self-effacing, courteous and unpretentious, their on-field understanding bordered on the telepathic. Brooking was the more accomplished of the two, but as he once acknowledged: 'I couldn't operate properly without Dev. He does all my running, and has the skill and awareness to be in the right places and to give me right return passes.'

Both were natural right-footed players but both gave the impression that they were born favouring the left. Referring to the number of 'one-footed' professional footballers, Brooking once said: 'The problem [in their development years as schoolboys] is that there are a lot more matches for kids nowadays, as opposed to the informal kick-arounds we used to have. It is more difficult to practise or experiment in a match situation. I was right-footed, for instance, and my dad told me to work on my weaker foot, so I did. I must have spent a whole summer playing with my left. If you are playing informally, for enjoyment, you can do that. You can't in matches, no matter how many you play in a week. When a kid tries something in a match, and it goes wrong, he won't try it again. That's why if you are one-footed these days, you tend to stay that way.'

Devonshire had been an outside-right initially but felt restricted there and was switched to the left side of midfield. 'It gave me the scope to move inside and use my right foot to cut across my opponents,' he says. 'It meant that I had virtually the full width of the pitch to work in.'

It was on the left side that West Ham, with Devonshire and Brooking supported by the attacking instincts of Frank Lampard from the left-back spot, were liable to cause teams the most damage. Of the three, Devonshire was the one who covered the most ground, as Brooking indicated with his comment about Dev doing 'all' his running for him. An exaggeration, obviously, but Brooking tended to operate in short, sporadic bursts, whereas Devonshire seemed to be on the move all the time. Devonshire's style, an extension of his restlessness as a person, complemented that of the laid-back Brooking perfectly. Of Devonshire, John Lyall once said: 'The way he runs at people must frighten them to death. I've seen him get the ball on the edge of our penalty area, run 50 or 70 yards with it, and still come back for more. I don't know where he gets his energy from.'

Ron Greenwood had a theory that Devonshire, the son of a former Crystal Palace, Chester and Brentford winger (Les), was motivated by his memories of his start in the game, when he played in semi-professional football for Southall and worked as a fork-lift truck driver. Greenwood said: 'He realises what a good life football is because he can make comparisons. It wouldn't be a bad idea if apprentices at every club were made to work on a factory floor or a building site for six months. It would give them a new set of values.'

Interestingly, Brooking's inner drive to be a professional footballer was not as strong. He was brighter academically than Devonshire had been, gaining 12 O-level GCEs and two A-levels at school, and then undertaking a business studies course from which he picked up diplomas in commerce, economics, statistics and accounts. It was not long before he started his own business, a plastic comb-binding company, and even in those days he could have been easily mistaken for a young executive. Throughout his entire career, in fact, Brooking, intelligent, articulate and a man with a broad view of life, stood out from the rest. He certainly did not fit the professional-footballer stereotype as well as Devonshire. Off the field, the latter's main interest outside his family was horse-racing; he loved a bet, and it was rare to see him arriving at the training ground without a copy of *Sporting Life* under his arm. Brooking was rather more eclectic. Such was his urbane image that his West Ham team-mates nicknamed him

'Hadleigh' after the refined, typically English gentleman portrayed in the popular TV drama series at that time.

In an interview during his early days at West Ham, Brooking said: 'Sometimes, the lads will be having an argument about something or other in the dressing-room, and then someone will say "Ask Trevor, he'll know." So they ask me, and if I don't know the answer – well, you can imagine what happens next, can't you? It's the same when I say something a bit profound. "Oh, look at him giving us all his long words and his English vocabulary." They tease me unmercifully at times, but I don't mind – it's all in good fun.'

To a great extent, the way Brooking came across off the field, as a man for whom there were more important things in life than football, was reflected in his languid style of play. Indeed, Brooking, who joined the Hammers as a wing-half but was also played at centre-forward, initially found it so difficult to come to terms with the sense of purpose and competitiveness required of top-level players that, for all his talent, West Ham had him on the transfer list for more than six months when he was in his early 20s, and he himself was on the verge of quitting the game. He has said: 'I had been in and out of the team and, quite frankly, my confidence was non-existent.

'My contract at West Ham was not that good and I talked to Hilkka [his wife] about getting out of the game completely. I would play in reserve games and think I was playing well enough to be in the first team. But when I wasn't, I thought: "Crikey, maybe you don't have what it takes to be a professional footballer anyway." It was all a matter of confidence. I seemed to be getting nowhere fast and I thought that if I gave up football and went into something else, like accountancy, I could establish myself in a couple of years.'

In later years, the memory of how close Brooking came to taking that step will have caused any West Ham diehard to break out in a cold sweat. Needless to say, it would have been the same with his West Ham managers, Ron Greenwood and John Lyall.

Here is how they looked back on Brooking's years at Upton

Park. Greenwood said: 'Brooking was a tall, angular centre-forward when he started to make an impression. He was very promising and I felt he had the talent for a worthwhile career, but he was inconsistent and, as Arthur Rowe [the former Tottenham manager] used to say, he "needed a squib up his backside". He was elegant, even in those days, but he was too casual and sometimes even lethargic. That was his style and I knew I would have to take him as he was.

'But there was certainly a doubt or two about him. We even put him on the transfer list one summer with an asking fee of £67,000. The only enquiry, though, came from Ted Bates [Southampton's manager] and even he couldn't make up his mind. Ted asked everybody about Brooking, but he still hadn't come to a decision by the start of the season. Then, after an indifferent start, I gave Trevor his chance and he took it well. He had got married by then, which is often a good thing for a young player. He was a more responsible person and it showed in his game.

'Brooking went on improving with age. He grew in stature, his personality rounded off, and he thought more about the game. He developed, in short, into a midfield player of the very highest quality. But his floppy ankles remained. His ankles were loose – floppy – and they posed a problem when it came to shooting. Unless he locked his ankle and hit right through, the ball was liable to go anywhere. I used to say to him: "Have you got your handbag with you?" It was part code, part private joke, a reminder to keep his ankle locked.

'But those floppy ankles had their uses. Their flexibility meant he could screw round the ball and get some wonderful angles.

'Brooking had many qualities including, importantly, a strong personality and natural authority. He could see a game as a whole, the complete picture, and was always quick to spot an opposition weakness. He was the best runner with the ball since Bobby Charlton. He knew when to carry the ball and when to let go. Brooking would also involve himself in a movement at just the right moment and, once in possession, he was very difficult to knock off the ball. He was an expert screener. He could play one-touch football with the best and his angles were usually just right. He knew when to let the ball run, often beating a man without making contact – and sometimes, just sometimes, he headed the ball!'

John Lyall said: 'I'd known Trevor since he came to us as an academically gifted schoolboy. His development was slow. He didn't find the physical side of training easy, although he would never give in. If I gave the players a five-mile run, he would finish – no matter how long it took. I said to Trevor more than once: "Okay, Trevor, the others have finished, you can stop now." He'd glare at me and say: "I'll finish."

'He had a competitive edge to his game that not too many people appreciated. But it was his determination to succeed that eventually made him such a great player.

'He was the classic improviser. Many players have one particular skill that they call upon repeatedly in given situations. Trevor had two or three for most situations. That, plus his knack of playing the ball as late as possible, made him a very difficult man to mark successfully.

'If I wanted to demonstrate a simple move in training, I would often use Trevor. Of course, he could do it the way I wanted but he could also do it his own way and often twice as efficiently. If I asked him to lay the ball off with the inside of his foot, he might instead lay it off with the outside of the other foot. It was all a bit tongue-in-cheek on his part. He knew exactly what I wanted, but he also knew that he was good enough to improvise.

'I remember scratching my head on more than one occasion and asking myself: "Why have I got *him* to demonstrate?"

'He had a wonderful touch and great awareness. Most players would try to anticipate what he was going to try to do with the ball. Trevor would sense their positioning and reaction, and respond accordingly.

'Some coaches used to tell me that he wasn't very quick but once he had swept past a defender, rarely would he get caught by the same player. He had aggression too, another facet of his game not widely acknowledged. Sometimes I'd say to Billy

Bonds or Geoff Pike in training: "Get after him and show him who's boss." Trevor would just get more competitive in his attitude and hold them off. I'd say to them afterwards: "You didn't do it," and they'd say: "We couldn't get near him."'

That was exactly the message Arsenal were left to contemplate after they had faced Brooking and Devonshire in the 1980 FA Cup final.

On the morning of the final, Brooking – English football's Mr Nice Guy – was the target of a remarkable newspaper attack by Brian Clough. It was not unusual, of course, for the Nottingham Forest manager, a man with an outstanding awareness of how to reap the financial benefits of the media's thirst for attention-grabbing headlines, to come out with something outspoken and controversial, not to say perverse. But even by his standards the brickbats he fired at Brooking that day, as the player was preparing for one of the biggest matches of his life, were disconcerting to say the least. In an article in the *Daily Express*, Clough, focusing on Brooking's elegant, laid-back style, expressed the view that, while the West Ham star 'floated like a butterfly', he also 'stung like one'.

He added: 'I have never had a high opinion of him as a player. He has been lucky enough to become a member of teams that he shouldn't really have had a sniff at. I believe that his lack of application, and that of other players like him, have meant relegation for West Ham in the past and their failure to win promotion this time [the Hammers had finished the season fifth in the Second Division]. Wembley is made for a player like Alan Devonshire. He is young, in form and full of confidence. Brooking will only be able to have an influence on this Cup final when Devonshire or another of his willing team-mates has battled to win it at the front or at the back so that he can pick it up in midfield.'

No doubt Clough himself will have argued that the 13th-minute Brooking goal that enabled the Hammers to achieve that surprise 1–0 win over their First Division rivals did much to illustrate his point. The goal belonged as much to Devonshire as it did to Brooking, as he had done the most to create the necessary space in the Gunners' redoubtable defence with a superb run down the left, which took him past both Brian Talbot and Pat Rice. Having got round the back of the Arsenal defence, Devonshire produced a fine cross from the dead-ball line. This is the sort of cross that defenders fear the most because the ball is swinging away from them and they have the dilemma of whether to 'attack' it or stay where they are.

In this particular instance, things went from bad to worse for the Gunners. Brooking said: 'Pat Jennings [the Arsenal keeper] just got a touch and the ball flew to David Cross on the right side of the box. Dave's shot was blocked by Willie Young and came out to Stuart Pearson, who was at a fairly tight angle on the right. Stuart instinctively tried a shot, scooping the ball across the box instead of at goal, and I realised I had only to reach it with my head to score. I fell backwards and managed to steer the ball goalwards. I knew it was a goal as soon as I connected. I had a quick look at the referee to see there was no offence and I hared off towards the left touchline with arms raised. I don't know why I went in that direction, there were few West Ham fans in that part of the stadium. Billy Bonds grabbed me, and his first words to me were: "What are you doing scoring with your head?" It was only the third or fourth time I had ever scored with my head.'

However, the most important point about Brooking was surely that he played with his head.

Clough's remarks about his approach to the game physically had never been lost on Brooking, who became so sensitive about his style of play (or rather how it was perceived) that being described as 'elegant' eventually caused him to cringe. He knew from an early age that he was not sharp and assertive enough, and he was also made aware that he could be easily knocked off his feet. 'Ron Greenwood once asked me why I kept falling over during my matches,' Brooking said. 'It happened so often that the other players called me "Cyril" after the Carpet King, Cyril Lord, because I was always on the floor. The only explanation I could offer was that I had a long stride at the time and perhaps I was off balance more than I should have been.'

He did strive to overcome these problems. One way in which he tackled them was to work with Len Heppell, a former professional ballroom dancing champion from Hexham, County Durham. Heppell, the father-in law of West Ham striker Bryan 'Pop' Robson, was highly respected among British football's more enlightened professionals for his advice on how they could become quicker, better balanced and more dynamic.

At West Ham the first player to sing his praises, apart from Robson, was Bobby Moore, who once said: 'Lenny told me I ran like a coat-hanger – upright – and when I looked at myself on TV I saw he was right. I had been told 15 years earlier than I should "stand big" to make myself look tall and commanding. But this made my running harder and slower. Lenny talked me into rolling my shoulders but not my body. He also got on to me about turning. He told me to turn like the ballroom-dancers – head first.

'To me, it was magic. It was something I wish I had heard years before, because my turning and speed of movement improved 100 per cent. It was a bit late for me, but Lenny was helping the others. He told Trevor Brooking exactly the opposite to me. Trevor was too relaxed. Easy-ohsy, flopping here, flopping there. Lenny tensed him up. Put some *oomph* in him. Next thing, Trevor's in the England team.'

Brooking, who made his England début in 1974 against Argentina, also felt that Heppell had played a major part in that breakthrough. He said, 'He [Heppell] thought I was too lacka-daisical in my movements, and said that this was because I was a casual, relaxed person off the field. He noticed I have a ten-dency to lounge around on chairs instead of sitting up properly, and believed this was an indication of my general attitude and, on his advice, I tried to make myself sharper.'

But Brooking was never going to be like Billy Bremner or Alan Ball, and West Ham were more than happy to accept him for what he was. Moore summed it up perfectly when he said, 'Any halfway decent side should be able to cater for one luxury player. Look at Trevor Brooking – a fabulous luxury for West Ham to have in their team. If his name had been Netzer or

Gerson or Rivera we would all have been crying out for an English player like him. But because he was English, we complained that he didn't run about enough or didn't tackle hard enough.'

In that respect, the irony of Brian Clough's action in putting the verbal boot in on Brooking on FA Cup final day was that he had once tried to sign him. It happened in 1973 when Clough, then Derby's manager, offered £400,000 to buy both Brooking and Bobby Moore. Clough had already been in touch with Moore privately, and Moore, viewing Clough as the ideal man to help him achieve greater success at club level, had no hesitation in expressing his interest in joining forces with him. The next step for Clough was to approach Greenwood. Their conversation in Greenwood's office went something like this.

Clough: 'I want to sign Bobby Moore and Trevor Brooking.'

Greenwood: 'You can't be serious.'

Clough: 'Every man's got a price.'

Greenwood: 'Look, there's no point in our continuing this conversation.'

Clough: 'Well, if I can't have Moore, can I have Brooking, and if I can't have Brooking, can I have Moore?'

Greenwood: 'They're not available, Brian.'

According to Greenwood, Clough carried on as if he hadn't heard him, and the amount of money Clough said Derby were prepared to pay was rising by the minute. Greenwood eventually agreed to put the proposition to the West Ham board. They backed Greenwood by turning it down, and Greenwood never heard from Clough on the matter again – not surprising in view of the fact that Clough sensationally resigned from Derby shortly afterwards.

When Brooking learned of Clough's attempt to buy him, his reaction was rather different to Moore's. In his autobiography – it was simply called *Trevor Brooking*, and published in 1981 – Brooking said: 'I cannot say I would have relished the idea of working with Brian Clough. I am not the type of player who would take to public criticism too kindly. I am like Trevor Francis in personality, and I know that Trevor [who became

Britain's first £1 million player when Clough bought him for Nottingham Forest] has not been too enraptured about some of the things Clough has said about him. Clough can be kind one minute, harsh and destructive the next. I am afraid I would take more notice of his strictures than his praise. Some players need this abrasive treatment and respond to it. I do not.'

The attitude towards him at Upton Park had always been something else. He was part of the family, not just because he was a local player who had graduated through the Upton Park youth system, but also because he encapsulated all the good 'habits' that Greenwood strove to instil into his players in both technical ability and conduct. If ever there was a player born to play for West Ham, it was Trevor Brooking. Even when things were not going well for him at the club in 1971, his fourth year as a member of the first-team squad, and he was on the transfer list, he did not truly want to leave.

'I appreciated that they had been good to me and helped me enormously. They weren't the only club who had wanted to sign me when I left school, but the big difference between them and the rest was that they were so conscious of making sure that I safeguarded myself against the prospect of being forced to do something else for a living. They cared a great deal about my further education – in fact, they encouraged it.

'In those days, the first-team seemed light years away. West Ham then were noted for their youth policy. When I joined them just after the European Cup-Winners' Cup final [in July 1965] I remember thinking about the competition I faced. I was a wing-half in those days, and quite apart from Bobby Moore, Martin Peters and Geoff Hurst – all primarily left-halves then – there were also youngsters like Trevor Dawkins and Bobby Howe, who were both spoken about as great prospects, and a lad called Pete Deadman, who went on to become an England amateur international.

'But it was a great club to be at. They had some great players and they also had some great characters. Take Johnny "Budgie" Byrne. I was an apprentice pro when he joined the club from Crystal Palace and I still remember his first words to me. I was complaining to another apprentice about the amount of tax I paid, and Budgie just said: "I shouldn't worry about it if I were you. I pay more in tax than the two of you earn."'

The put-down will have bothered the other player more than it did Brooking, who did not need to rely as heavily on the game for his livelihood as many others, a point which was to be illustrated by the success that Brooking would later achieve as a businessman and TV pundit.

Recalling his feelings about being in the West Ham reserves for much of the 1970–71 season, he said: 'Playing in front of 200 or 300 people in reserve matches is soul-destroying. Some clubs keep their first-team squad happy by paying all of them the squad rate, whether they are in the team or not. Rather than accept this "non-person" role, I think I would retire from the game and go into business. Many players go from club to club in order to protect their status as full-time professionals but many of them would be better off taking a job outside the game and playing non-league football part-time.'

Fortunately, thoughts that this might happen to Brooking were crushed early in the 1971–72 season: 'They [West Ham] had been beaten in their first two matches, and a reshuffle brought me in. Tommy Taylor had been filling the number 10 position, with Alan Stephenson partnering Bobby Moore in defence. If Tommy had succeeded as a midfield player, I might have left the club or even gone out of the game. But after the opening matches, Greenwood moved him back to centre-half and dropped Stephenson. I was recalled to midfield and played there for the rest of the season. Crisis over.'

Brooking's inclusion in the side coincided with a run in which the Hammers lost only once in 12 matches, and led to his being voted 'Hammer of the Year' by the club's supporters – an honour which he would achieve a record three times in succession. 'I also started my own business and gained my one and only England Under-23 cap,' he adds. 'So that season was very much a turning point in my career.'

One of the greatest pleasures for Brooking-followers concerned his passing, an element of his game in which he himself derived the most satisfaction. He was particularly proud of his ability to bend the ball around defenders with his left foot.

'When I kick with my left foot, I usually bend the ball from left to right involuntarily. The ball curls like an in-swinger to a right-handed batsman. I find I wrap my foot around the ball, producing a swinging effect which does not occur when I am kicking with my right foot. I think most left-footed players can bend the ball more than a right-footed player. With me, it is probably a legacy of training to be a two-footed player. My left, being the weaker foot, struck the ball in a different way to my right. You can see it when I take my boots off – the left foot is curled inwards more than my right.'

To Brooking, one of the most notable of his passes was the devastating cross from the right wing to the far post that brought Ted MacDougall a goal in a match against Newcastle. 'In my first few years at West Ham I often drifted towards the wings, and carried out the role of a winger. However, as the team became stronger all-round and started to include other players who could get in on the by-line – like Alan Devonshire, Geoff Pike and Patsy Holland – I was able to concentrate more on getting in the box and scoring goals.'

In that department, too, Brooking, with more than 100 goals for the club, was a player one couldn't help but admire. That did not mean, however, that Clough was out on a limb in his criticism of him. One who also wanted to see him sweat a bit more was Don Revie. Brooking, thinking back to his experience of working with Revie in the England squad, said: 'He told me I could be a regular member of his side if I ironed out some faults. He thought I should be more aggressive and try to dictate play more than I did. "Midfield is the most important part of the team," he said. "That's where it all starts. You've got a tendency to drift out of games. You drift along with the game instead of shaping it the way you want."' Brooking looked upon this as 'well-meaning advice', and liked to think that he subsequently improved. But, the one thing that Brooking did not change was his belief that football should be played in the 'right way' – the West Ham way. The first page of his autobiography said it all.

'Standards have declined,' he wrote, 'and there are fewer skilled players in the game than when I started as an apprentice 16 years ago, on 24 July 1965. Football has become more a business and less a sport. Players have become more regimented. But I am lucky to have worked under two managers [Greenwood and Lyall] who value skill and who have allowed me to express whatever skill I have.'

Brian Scovell of the *Daily Mail*, his book collaborator and a self-confessed Brooking fan, spoke for every West Ham supporter when he wrote: 'Trevor Brooking is a gentleman in a rough game – an authentic English hero. As football has become fiercer, more competitive and less enjoyable, he has carried on delighting us with his skill. He is an honest player in a sport that can at times be very dishonest. He has never been involved in any scandal and his [disciplinary] record is beyond reproach.'

So there can be no arguments that Brooking, who was awarded the MBE in 1981, does not merit a place in the West Ham dream team. In his more reflective moments even Brian Clough would surely be moved to agree that Trevor Brooking was a dream footballer.

*　　　　*　　　　*

Trevor Brooking was 35 when he elected to call it a day as a professional footballer in May 1984. He could easily have gone on longer, but wanted to bow out at the top; however, many believe that the decision was influenced to some extent by the fact that Alan Devonshire, a colleague who could have played a bigger part than most in helping Brooking prolong his career as a top-class performer, had been forced out of the team with a serious knee injury.

Devonshire himself looks back on the timing of Brooking's retirement as one of the biggest compliments he has ever had. 'I think Trevor was going to stay on for another year,' Devonshire says.

At the time of the injury, which occurred in an FA Cup tie at home to Wigan in January 1984 and was to put him out of action for virtually the whole of the next 19 months, the 28-year-old Devonshire was producing what he considered to be the best form of his West Ham career. Certainly, in view of the brilliant rapport between the two men in their previous seven seasons together, Brooking must have wished that it was possible to stop the clock until Dev was ready to step back on to the scene again – even though Dev was not quite the same player that he had been before.

By that time Devonshire had lost some of his pace, and therefore some of his ability to carry the ball past opponents. But against that, he added a new dimension to his career by concentrating more on one- and two-touch passing. Indeed, though he himself has mixed feelings about his effectiveness then, many would suggest that the injury led to his becoming a more complete player. Frank McAvennie and Tony Cottee would have been the last players to disagree with that view, considering the high number of goals Dev set up for them in the 1985–86 season, when the Hammers finished in their highest-ever First Division position.

Devonshire continued to play for the club until May 1990, when Billy Bonds gave him a free transfer and he moved to Watford. Then 34, he believes that but for the injury and its effect on his mobility and stamina he could easily have played for the Hammers for another two or three years. He also feels that the Hammers fans never really saw the best he was capable of producing for them. Maybe so, but Devonshire – both before and after his long lay-off – was still on a higher plateau than most other British midfield players; and as far as midfield partnerships are concerned, the same could be said of his link with Brooking. Here's how Devonshire looks back on that link.

'We just hit it off together straight away. I knew his strengths and he knew mine, and our minds just seemed to work together.

'The pity of it was that we only played together on one occasion for England [the 1–1 draw against Ireland at Wembley in May 1980]. He was on the right and I was on the left and we just weren't in close enough contact with each other. Actually, England played me as more or less a left-winger, but I wasn't a winger, I was a midfield player and at West Ham I used to be able to go anywhere I wanted to.

'When I had the ball, and maybe had two players on me, he would often make a little run in front of me, inviting me to thread it through them for him, and you knew that nine times out of ten, the ball would be safe with him. It did not really matter if he was tightly marked because although Trevor did not have much pace, he was a big lad and would get the yard or half-yard he needed to take the ball by rolling his backside into people and knocking them off balance.

'I did not have his physical strength, but I had pace – a lot of pace. That was the area in which Trevor and I probably differed the most. I remember an American coach coming over to England to study players at different clubs and singling me out as one of the most unusual. He said that it was not so much my pace that had impressed him, but the way I controlled and varied it. The way he put it was that I had a number of running "gears". When I picked the ball up and saw a defender 10 or 15 yards away moving towards me to close me down, I would slow down. As he got closer to me, I'd slow down even more – and then, just when he might have thought he was going to get the ball, I'd suddenly accelerate clear of him. I used to beat a lot of people like that. It was one of the reasons why I took so much stick. I know that a lot of the people who kicked me didn't mean to hurt me. As I say, I used to entice them in and get caught by late tackles.

'I think I was possibly fitter than Trevor, too. It was just the way we were made, a natural thing. I'm a naturally fit person, and for me, being able to to run all over the park, up and down, up and down – well, it was the best feeling in the world. I don't think I could have been a lazy player, I had to be active all the time. So that was one way in which I could complement Trevor. He used to sit in the "hole" [the space between the midfielders and strikers] and as I would be deeper than him nine times out of ten, I could play the ball up to him, and then go forward outside him to give him the option of returning it to me closer to the goal.

'When I played the ball to Trevor I had to play it to his feet, or thereabouts, I wouldn't expect him to run 10 or 15 yards to get the ball. But he knew he could do either with me, which was a bonus for both of us. In my own case, the opposition did not know whether to get tight on me or stand off me.'

Of all the wonderful images of Devonshire at his best, the manner in which he helped set up that 1980 FA Cup final goal for Brooking is inevitably the one that springs to mind most readily. But when you ask Devonshire to pinpoint his best West Ham matches, he has no hesitation in plumping for the semi-final replay against Everton at Elland Road. Devonshire had played well in the 1–1 draw between the two teams at Villa Park, despite the unsettling effect of having a penalty awarded against him for an innocuous-looking challenge on Brian Kidd, from which the Everton striker opened the scoring. Kidd, Everton's best attacker, was later sent off for a foul on Ray Stewart, thus causing him to miss the replay four days later. Everton attempted to spike West Ham's guns, too, by assigning John Gidman, their England right-back, to carry out a man-marking job on Devonshire. But in addition to scoring a superb first goal in West Ham's 2–1 victory, Devonshire's bursts with the ball down the left flank made him appear as if he was playing Everton almost on his own.

Dev says: 'I actually won the man-of-the-match award in both games and ended up with two televisions as prizes, but the second game was really special for me. It was one of those days when I could have run all day and nobody would have been able to catch up with me – nobody. I was carrying the ball into crossing positions right from as far back as the edge of our box and I can't honestly remember one Gidman tackle on me. I just felt like Superman that day – I've never experienced anything quite like it.'

Inevitably, his goal, the result of a slick exchange of passes which put him behind the Everton defence, and a shot under the keeper's body when Dev was struggling to keep his balance after having his heels clipped, was particularly memorable.

'It was the greatest feeling of my life. When Everton equalised, it was the worst feeling, but that goal was unquestionably the best moment of my career. My dad's got it on video and I have to laugh when I watch it because when Trevor came over to congratulate me, I was so excited that I sort of brushed him aside. I could easily have done four laps of honour, you know.

'As for the final, well I felt I let myself down. I know people say: "Oh, you beat two players and got the cross in for the goal," but, actually, I was disappointed with my display. I didn't feel right. It was probably the only time in my career that I felt under pressure. I'd attracted a lot of attention with that unbelievable game in the semi-final replay and it seemed to me that people were expecting too much of me. I remember discussing it with Trevor on the eve of the final. "I ain't half taken the pressure off you," I said. "Nobody's talking about what you are going to do at Wembley – it's all about what I am going to do."

'It just got to me, which was weird because that was the only time it ever happened to me. I wasn't a cocky lad – I did not believe in shouting my mouth off and telling people what I could do – but I was extremely self-confident. I never worried about the opposition. Football-wise, I didn't worry about anything.

'Even if I had the ball in my own penalty area, I found it difficult to boot it out. No matter what match I was playing in, my first thought was to pass it out. Touch wood, there weren't many times that I lost the ball in a dangerous area, but maybe that was down to the fact that I had enough confidence not to panic on the ball.'

At this point, it is pertinent to ask where that confidence came from. Devonshire was 20 when he arrived at West Ham as a £5,000 buy from the Isthmian League club, Southall. It was not the first time he had been involved with a Football League club. Previously he had been with QPR, eventually leaving as a result of a disagreement with their youth team coach, and when he was 16 he spent a year as an amateur player at Crystal Palace.

'I just trained with them and played for the junior team on a Saturday. I was promised a professional contract when I got to 17, but about a month before I was due to sign, Bert Head [the manager] got the sack and was replaced by Malcolm Allison and that was that for me.

'What Allison did straight away was trim the playing staff – at that time Palace must have had some 50 professionals and apprentices – and I got the chop without him ever having seen me play. I was very disillusioned, I must admit. In fact, I did not play at all for six months after that. But then my father persuaded me to go to Southall.'

Life was not easy for Devonshire, who got married at 19 and worked as a fork-lift driver at the Hoover factory. 'They were days when we had to watch the pennies, never mind the pounds. We could just about afford a small flat. Even then, signing for West Ham was a gamble because I was earning more money at the Hoover factory and West Ham only offered me a one-year contract. But I thought: "Yeah, let's go for it." From that point, things happened really quickly for me. I was only there for about four weeks before I was in the team.'

It is easy to see why the West Ham fans found it so easy to relate to him. Even at the height of his career, Devonshire though nothing of 'going to work' from his west London home on the London Underground.

'I knew what it was like to get up at seven in the morning and work until five for not a lot of money,' he recalls, 'so I loved every minute of being a full-time professional footballer. I can't believe that some players can't work their socks off all the time because, at the end of the day, you're only working two or three hours a day and you should be able to give 100 per cent to that. It irritates me when I hear players moaning about their contracts and things like that. They should be concentrating on going out and working their nuts off.

'The way West Ham trained was great for me, because you did so much of the day-to-day work with the ball. There was a lot of one- and two-touch stuff, and if you are doing that every day your touch and control must improve. It was hard work, much harder than if we had been doing five-mile runs all the time. When you are just running it gets boring and you look for excuses to slow down. It's different when you are working with the ball, you forget about the little aches and pains and actually find yourself working twice as hard.

'The other big plus for me in joining West Ham was the way Trevor and Billy Bonds looked after me. In the case of Bonzo, playing with him was like having my dad on the pitch with me. It was impossible for me to respect anyone as much as I respected those two boys. In all the years we played together, I don't think we ever said one bad word to each other.'

But Devonshire was also helped by his experiences of playing for Southall. Strange as it might seem, the confidence he showed at West Ham could be said to have been developed because of those experiences, not in spite of them. Devonshire acknowledges the point when discussing how matches for Southall, with and against a number of players older and bigger than himself, sharpened his competitive edge.

'In no way is it as physical in the First Division or Premiership as it is in non-league football – I don't care what anyone says. I found it a lot tougher physically in the Isthmian League, if only because the standard of refereeing wasn't as good. If you are a good player, you quickly become a marked man.

'There was not a lot of me and I got kicked all the time. But the more I got kicked, the more wound up I became – not in the sense of retaliating, but getting my own back through my performance. In one Cup match against Boreham Wood, I actually came back on to the field after being carried off at half-time with stud marks all the way down my calves, both of which were bleeding. I thought: "Sod them – they're asking for trouble." We eventually won 2–1.

'I don't know why I had this streak in me. Skill-wise, people could argue that I was like my father [whose Football League career as a Brentford, Chester and Crystal Palace winger spanned six years just after the war]. But I always remember my mum saying that while he could play, he did not have the necessary "bottle". Maybe her saying that made me more determined to be different.

'I learned the hard way in that league. In the year or so I was at Southall, from 17 or 18, I picked up more knowledge from playing than any coach could ever give me. It got to the stage where I would have two men marking me and had to work out how to combat things like that myself.

'I always thought a lot about the game. After a match I'd discuss everything I'd done with my dad, and even when I went to bed that night, I'd be thinking about various situations and how I could have done better.'

Hence the fact that Devonshire was able to shrug aside the horror of his injury, which seriously undermined what he and most others considered to be his greatest attribute. The injury – extensive ligament damage in his right knee – was caused by an accidental collision with a Wigan player as Dev attempted to control a difficult pass from Alvin Martin. He recalls: 'They took me into the treatment room and when the doctor lifted my knee up, it was just waving around – there was nothing there to hold it together. He said to me: "We'll have to get you an operation," and at this, I just panicked. I'd never had an operation in my whole life. I actually said to him, "No, it's okay, I'll get up," but when I tried to do so the knee obviously gave way.'

After the operation Devonshire's knee was in plaster for three months and by the time he was due to start his gruelling rehabilitation programme – at an army training camp in Leatherhead, Surrey – the muscles in his leg were virtually non-existent and he had lost more than a stone in weight.

'I stayed down there, in the officer's mess, for eight months. It wasn't great for my family – I was a horrible person to my family then – but I knew that I had to give it my best shot. I was 10st 10lb before my injury, but when I made my comeback I was 11st 10lb. All the extra weight had been put on through the work I had done on my lower body. I'd worked every day from 8.30 in the morning until 4.30 in the afternoon – I only stopped for lunch – and by the end of it all, I was probably fitter than I had ever been in my life.'

But the downside for Dev was that, while the knee was strong enough to withstand the physical demands of the game, it did not have the same mobility: 'As far as my pace was concerned, I lost 10 to 15 yards over 100 yards. I couldn't sprint. I could run at three-quarter pace, but as soon as I went to actually sprint the leg would not come through.

'Previously, whatever situation I was in, I knew I could get out of it just by stepping up a gear. Now, I couldn't do that. I was able to kid people to some extent – some opposing players would still be wary of me taking them on, and I could beat them by dropping my shoulder to pretend that I was going to take the ball past them on their outside and then just come inside. But generally I had to play a lot differently, and although people felt I was doing well, I knew deep down that I wasn't the same player. It hurt, to be honest with you.'

It's a pity that Devonshire, one of the most likeable of star players, does not always see himself as others see him. 'It's a great feeling to have people come up to you and say how much pleasure you have given them. One or two of them actually wanted to kiss my feet. It shows you how much football means to people. The West Ham fans, in particular, have been tremendous to me. I'm sure that some of them realised that I was a different player after my injury, but not once did they give me any stick over it.

'Not long ago I was at a testimonial dinner and a man in his 40s came up to me and said: "My dad is really shy but he badly wants to meet you." So I went over, and the old man was really choked up. I don't know whether he was going senile or not, but he was putting me in the same category as people like Pele. "At West Ham you were far and away the best player I have ever seen," he said. I must say I got a lot of pleasure from that, and it reminded me of one of the reasons why I never wanted to leave West Ham.

'I could have left when I was in my mid-20s – a lot of clubs were interested in me then – but at West Ham you just felt that everybody was behind you and you were really appreciated. John Lyall would tell me if any clubs had made an offer for me because he didn't want me to find out about it in the papers. "To be honest, John," I'd say, "I'm happy where I am – I don't want to go, unless you want to sell me." He'd say: "Oh no – no chance."'

No amount of money could compensate for things like that.

CHAPTER 9

Ronnie Boyce

Ronnie Boyce, the quiet man of West Ham's outstanding FA Cup and European Cup-Winners' Cup teams of the 1960s, says that he was never frustrated by his unobtrusive role among the likes of Moore, Hurst and Peters.

But, says Boyce, his father was. 'Dads are like that – they all want to see their sons in the limelight, don't they? He always used to get on to me about not trying enough shots and things like that. I remember that one thing that got to him was the fact that, having worked hard to win the ball, I would then give a little five-yard ball to Mooro [Moore]. "Why do you keep giving the ball to Mooro?" he'd say. You know, my dad found it hard to understand what I did, especially when he saw Moore go on one of those great runs with the ball or play a 30- to 40-yard pass. My dad's attitude was "Why let Moore take all the glory when you can do things like that yourself?"'

But Boyce senior, who was the proprietor of a corner shop in East Ham, had no cause to complain about his son not standing out when the midfielder hit the first two goals in West Ham's epic 3–1 FA Cup semi-final victory over Manchester United at Hillsborough in 1964; when Boyce headed the injury-time goal which gave the Hammers their 3–2 win over Preston in the final; and when Boyce supplied the magnificent pass which enabled Alan Sealey to open the scoring in their European Cup-Winners' Cup final triumph over TSV Munich 1860 the following year.

Boyce himself likes to think that the old man will have been especially proud of him at the start of that Cup-Winners' Cup road, when he took over from the injured Moore as the Hammers' sweeper for the second-leg tie against Spartak Prague in Czechoslovakia and produced the best display of his career. West Ham, 2–0 up from the first leg, relied heavily on Boyce to limit Spartak's second victory to 2–1. On a night when the Hammers emphasised that they could be as dogged and unyielding under pressure as any team, the other hero was goalkeeper Jim Standen, who saved a penalty. But it was Boyce, who repeatedly frustrated the Czechs with his astute reading of the game, who attracted most of the plaudits.

In the *Evening Standard*, Bernard Joy, one of England's most respected football correspondents, wrote: 'If England manager Alf Ramsey still believes that he needs two midfield dynamos to run the team, then he must call on dark-haired, non-stop Ron Boyce of West Ham. And even if he no longer believes in the theory, he should still play the 21-year-old Boyce because he is not merely a worker, but is intelligent, skilful and determined. Boyce proved again in the Cup-Winners' Cup that he can hold his own in the highest class of football. He has emerged this season from being the quiet, self-effacing oil in the West Ham machine to being the very hub of the side. His comments about playing Bobby Moore's sweeper role behind the defence against Spartak were modest: "It wasn't difficult. All I had to do was move to where a gap looked like developing. My job was made easy by the way manager Ron Greenwood explained what had to be done."

'Yet Moore's absence was hardly noticed – and this was the very first time Boyce had ever attempted the role and only the second time he had played out of the forward line. The secret of West Ham's success is adaptability to different types of conditions, opponents and occasions. Boyce, as the prompter just behind the attack, or an extra half-back or, as yesterday, a deeper centre-half, is the man who transforms them on the field. If England are to win the World Cup in 1966, they must play six different countries in a fortnight. Boyce would help to give England flexibility in these situations.'

As England were to show, they already had more than enough of a West Ham influence with Moore, Peters and Hurst to achieve that feat. But at Upton Park, Boyce, who never did get a full England cap and gained only one at Under-23 level, was rated no less important than any of these three.

He was referred to as 'Ticker' because of his part in maintaining the heartbeat of the team. He was one of those players who tend to be held in greater esteem by their fellow professionals than by the public. He was the epitome of what people in football describe as a professionals' professional.

The attention of supporters is generally focused on the players on the ball, and it is not often that they appreciate the manner in which those players are being helped by the positioning of team-mates off it. Fellow professionals had an immensely high regard for this side of Boyce's game, the intelligence he showed in supporting colleagues in defence and attack. If a defender or midfield player burst forward – something that happened quite often in a team as attack-conscious as West Ham – you could bet that Boyce would fill in for him. He was equally willing to present himself as an outlet to anyone in trouble on the ball, repeatedly making it easy for the player to get the ball to him and then re-directing it to someone else in a similarly efficient, straightforward manner.

To the general public, Boyce came across as functional and unexciting. But his discipline certainly made him a tremendous team player. 'There were so many good players around at the time and I think you were conscious of that,' Boyce explains. 'Ron Greenwood did not mind you trying something different, but there was a difference between that and abusing the game. If you took liberties – in my case, making unnecessary forward runs that left us exposed defensively – you would be the one to ultimately suffer.'

His discipline was also highlighted by the fact that, despite his defensive responsibilities, he rarely committed a reckless tackle and the only time his name appeared in a referee's notebook was when he was cautioned in a reserve game.

'The referee wanted to have a little word with me and I said something to him because I thought things were all jovial and what have you,' recalls Boyce. 'He said, "Say that to me again and I'll book you," and, thinking that he was still messing about, I did. I can't even remember what I said, to be honest.

'You were brought up at West Ham to play the game the right way. There were some midfield players around who would think nothing of having a dig at you, even off the ball. You'd be watching the play, and all of a sudden someone would give you a little whack on the ankles as he was running past. It wasn't in my nature to do that. I would never make a tackle if I felt I couldn't get the ball without harming someone. Yeah, that was me all over.'

As for Greenwood's assessment of Boyce's value to the team, he might well have had the player in mind when he once said: 'Simplicity is genius'. In his book, Greenwood, speaking about the players who formed the axle of the Hammers' successful Cup side of the mid-'60s, added Boyce's name to those of Johnny Byrne, Moore, Peters and Hurst. He said: 'Boyce's inclusion here will be the unexpected name for many, but he was vital to us.

'Arsenal had been keen on him when I was at Highbury [when Greenwood was assistant manager there and Boyce was a schoolboy]. I even interviewed him there and I can only thank my lucky stars that I did not persuade him to stay. Boyce took over in midfield when Phil Woosnam left for Aston Villa and he really was exceptional. He was a first-class technician, a wily architect and a tireless worker – hence his nickname Ticker.

'He did everything simply but all the other players knew how valuable he was. He even shaped the way Peters, Moore and Hurst played. They depended on him more than most people realised. We could play Peters loose because we had Boyce as our springboard. Peters and Hurst could make their runs knowing that Boyce would always find them, usually with an early ball. And Moore knew that, whatever the pressure, Boyce would be available in front of him.

'Boyce read a game expertly, and this was always apparent in five-a-sides. Another player would make a perfectly good pass, with exactly the right weight and direction, but Ronnie would somehow intercept because he had read the passer's mind. You could sense everyone wondering: "How did he spot that?"'

No doubt the same thought crossed the minds of those who witnessed his extraordinary goal against Manchester City at Maine Road in March 1970, when City's keeper Joe Corrigan drop-kicked the ball up the field and Boyce – noting that the big man had left his net unguarded – volleyed it straight back and into the net from the halfway line. More often than not, however, Boyce exploited his ability in a more understated manner.

A former England schoolboy and youth international, he was only 17 when he made his first-team début against Preston at Upton Park in October 1960, and established himself in the side two seasons later. As a young player, he says that the Hammers winger, Malcolm Musgrove – who scored a hat-trick in Boyce's début game – was one of the senior professionals who had the biggest influence on him.

'He operated on the left, alongside the "chicken run" [the section of Upton Park where the Hammers' most partisan fans were situated] and if he wasn't having a good time he took so much stick from the crowd it wasn't true. But when he came in after the match, he always had a smile on his face. His attitude was: "Hey, it's not the end of the world – there's another game next week." I always admired him for that, and it was something that I tried to copy.

'I think I dealt with criticism quite well. I was the type who wanted to get on with everybody, and even if someone with no professional football experience came up to me to tell me about something he thought I was doing wrong, I would always give him the respect of at least listening to what he had to say. I would never say: "Oh, clear off, what do you know about it?"

'But for me, there was nothing worse than the occasional moment in a match when the place would be deathly quiet and all of a sudden you'd hear someone on the terraces shout: "Boyce, you're this" or "Boyce, you're that". It's funny when you look back on things like that, but the fact that I can still remember them shows you the effect they might have had on me.

'Ron Greenwood and John Lyall would say to me: "It's not going well for you, but what are you going to do about it? Are you going to hide?" I always thought of Musgrove at times like these.'

He also thought about the dedication of Moore. 'A great player who never stopped working on his game. People don't appreciate how much he practised his skills. Even when he'd won 100 England caps, he'd still go into the gym at West Ham after the normal training session and spend five or ten minutes just passing the ball against the wall.'

But even Moore did not have as long a career at Upton Park as Boyce. He spent 13 seasons as a player there, making 339 first-team appearances, and later had spells as first-team coach (under the management of both John Lyall and Billy Bonds), temporary manager (following the resignation of Lou Macari), youth team coach and finally chief scout.

Throughout all of his career, Boyce, modest and unassuming, provided an intriguing contrast with some of the leading lights with whom he was closely associated. In his early days, these included Terry Venables. He and Venables were good friends as youngsters. Venables, also an east London boy (he was born and raised in Dagenham), had the same birthday as Boyce (6 January 1943) and the pair played together in the England schoolboy and youth teams. For a while, Venables also trained with Boyce at West Ham. Boyce admired him for his gregarious personality and 'front' as much as for his ability. Even in those days, 'Venners' – a natural entertainer if ever there was one – stood out in any crowd. 'You never knew what he was going to get up to next,' Boyce says, recalling Venables' sense of showmanship on the field and his 'cheekie chappie' persona off it. 'The best story I have ever heard about him concerns an afternoon when he bumped into Martin Peters' wife, Kathy, on the underground. They were both going up to town, and the tube was packed. But as Kathy was getting off two or three stops before Terry, he shouted: "Don't leave me, please don't leave me . . . what about the kids?" Oh, he's a great character,' Boyce says, a shade enviously. 'It's great to see how far he has gone in life. Good luck to him.'

Boyce also provided an intriguing contrast with his West Ham midfield predecessor Woosnam, and not just because the latter, a Welsh international and West Ham's captain, appeared more of a flair-player. Greenwood had admired Woosnam greatly, especially the sense of responsibility Woosnam showed to the team, but made the point that this could be taken to the extreme. 'He [Woosnam] was to have a problem period caused by some of the very qualities that had made him such an asset,' Greenwood observed. 'He wanted to do everybody's work, and would even drop back and take the ball off his own defenders. He smothered the younger players and robbed them of their individuality. He "helped" them so much, they couldn't express themselves.' This was much less liable to happen with Boyce, who had the same ability to be of service to his colleagues as Woosnam, but was not as strong-minded and assertive. He gave them all the help they needed, but at the same time was happy to remain in the background. The irony is that he was a rather different player when he joined West Ham.

He recalls: 'I loved getting forward and scoring goals, but when I got into the first team they had so many attacking players that Ron Greenwood said to me, "Look, can you just sit in there?" That did not mean that I couldn't go forward, but my first responsibility was to take up a holding position in the middle of the park and concentrate on what could happen if the move broke down. Maybe I took it too literally, but as far as I was concerned, Ron Greenwood was in charge of the club and if he wanted me to do something, then I had to try my utmost to do it. It was as simple as that.'

To put it another way, Boyce found himself heading for a career as a member of the West Ham supporting cast. But in many ways this suited his personality and temperament. Certainly, one factor which made him perfect for the role of helping team-mates do their jobs properly was that he was a 'born worrier'. If anyone could see the dark cloud behind the silver lining of West Ham's irrepressibly adventurous approach to the game, and make sure the umbrellas were to hand, it was Boyce.

He admits: 'I'm a great worrier, always have been. I've been blessed with a wife who can take things in her stride, but with me – well, I remember that even at the height of my career at West Ham, I was always looking over my shoulder to see what youngsters were coming through to challenge for my first-team spot. This helped me in one way, it meant that I did not take anything for granted and pushed myself that little bit more. But I wish I could have been a bit more relaxed sometimes.'

It was perhaps typical of him that when West Ham allowed the FA Cup trophy (won against Fulham in 1975) to be displayed for a day or two in his father's shop, Boyce – anxious about having it there overnight – took it to a friend's house for safe-keeping under a bed. And when West Ham were playing at Upton Park on a Saturday, who else but Boyce would turn up some two and a half to three hours before the kick-off? 'You're uptight sitting at home before a match. My routine on a Saturday would be up at about nine o'clock, a walk in my local park, one cigarette, a bit of boiled fish and a walk to the ground to be there at 12.30-ish.' Boiled fish? 'Boiled fish – it was always boiled fish,' he says. 'It's all I could get down, really, to be honest.' So what did he do when he got to the ground? 'I'd just sit in the dressing-room and start getting changed an hour early. I had a routine – I'd go in the gym first, do a little bit in there, have a shower and get changed into my kit . . .' He pauses and shrugs. 'I couldn't sit at home – I had to be down there. I felt a lot better when I had arrived at the ground and was in the dressing-room.'

In addition to having a tendency to look for all potential areas in which his life could go wrong, another Boyce characteristic was his off-the-field public shyness, especially in front of men wielding pens and notebooks, microphones and TV cameras. 'I hated the media publicity side of things. I hated seeing my name and picture in print. Detested it,' he says.

'It shows you how bad I was that this was the thing I found the most difficult to handle when I was caretaker manager [between Lou Macari's resignation and the appointment of Billy Bonds in February 1990]. It was only for a week, and I didn't have any matches – all I had to do was supervise the coaching and training. But I didn't sleep a wink the whole week. On the first day, I can remember the press coming down to the ground. Oh, what a day that was. I had walked in after a training session and all the press lads were there. I thought, "What the bloody hell . . . ? Perhaps we've got a new manager." I asked what they were all doing there and someone said, "The club have put out a statement saying you're the caretaker manager." It was news to me. Nobody at the club had said a word to me about it. Anyway, the press – there are loads of them – are buzzing around, asking me questions, taking photographs, and to be honest with you, I'm feeling more and more uncomfortable by the minute.

'I knew I couldn't possibly be a manager – I knew it. Attracting that sort of attention would have been much too much for me. It was just the way I was. That night was terrible for me. I actually started worrying about what I'd said [to the media] and how it would be interpreted in the newspapers the next day. So at 5 a.m., I was out of bed and going down the road to get them all.'

This disarming self-consciousness is still prevalent in Boyce, as a small boy by the name of Luke can confirm. Boyce explains: 'My wife does a little bit of voluntary charity work with kids, and I go down on a Friday night to do some football coaching just to help her. There was a carnival in the town, so they decked out this open-topped lorry and arranged for all the kids to go on it dressed as Spice Girls. It was terrific – the kids loved it. As they were about to leave, one of them, an eight-year-old named Luke, asked me if I was coming on. "Oh no," I said. "I'm too shy." At this, he just shook his head and said: "You've played in front of 100,000 people at Wembley and yet you won't get on this lorry just for a drive around the town."'

But being on a football field, any football field, was different. When he was there, Boyce, through his intense concentration on the play and all its subtle tactical and strategic nuances, could easily get lost in a world of his own. Reading the ever-changing situations of a football match, anticipating how they were liable to evolve, was the name of the game for him. It had to be to some extent because he says, 'My left foot was useless and I didn't have great pace. Well, I suppose I was fairly quick, but I wasn't what you would call a natural athlete.' What he did have, though, were sound basic skills and, of course, a tremendous football brain. His grammar school education might not have yielded as much as he and his family hoped for in terms of academic qualifications (he took eight O-levels and failed all of them), but his education at West Ham, English football's thinking-man's club, produced better results. When Boyce talks about the part he played in helping West Ham function properly as a team, he might easily be discussing his moves in a game of chess.

'As I said earlier, I didn't have a lot of pace. So for me to get from A to B, it was a case of taking up a position where I could reach that position without leaving myself stranded if the ball didn't end up there. When you are asked to do a holding job in midfield, you know you're liable to be isolated and that even when your team have the ball and are attacking, you have to be aware of the positioning of the opposing team's midfielders and forwards, and what their counter-attacking options are. That's where the discipline comes in. If the ball's in a wide position, you can push across and make yourself available for a pass, and you can make a forward run occasionally. But in the attacking sense, you don't get too involved – you should be too busy thinking "Well, if it breaks down, they [the other team] might do this, or they could do that."'

Thus, life for Boyce on a football field was often a battle of wits, especially when he found himself in the position of being the last West Ham defender and had an opponent running at him with the ball or, even worse, was in a one-against-two situation. But at times like these, Boyce, with his ability to avoid panicking and to out-think opponents, was in his element. In those one-against-two situations, he was outstanding at deliberately adopting a stance that would invite the player on the ball to pass to his colleague and then sticking out a foot to prevent it reaching him. 'I don't like to talk about myself,' he says, 'but I tended to work out a lot of things for myself.'

In terms of his work on the ball and his effectiveness when involving himself in the team's attacking build-up play, some team-mates were inevitably easier to play with than others. Hence when you tell him he has been selected for the West Ham dream team to operate alongside Trevor Brooking and Alan Devonshire as the midfield anchor man, he feels duty bound to point out: 'I did not play with Trevor and Alan that often – I had most of my matches in the 1960s whereas they came to the fore in the 1970s – and when Trevor and I were in the team together, I did find him difficult to play with. Trevor was at an early stage of his development, of course, but I always remember that when you expected him to give you the ball, he would do something else. It was great for the team, but he did confuse you a little bit.

'But he was a great player, as was Dev. Alan was outstanding – I thought he had everything. Remember his pace? He loved picking the ball up deep and running at people with the ball. He'd often come into his own half to get the ball, and sometimes I would be telling him he should get further up the park. But even from those positions, he was liable to cause all kinds of problems for the opposing defence.'

Inevitably Boyce is even more enthusiastic about the West Ham dream team players from his own generation, notably Moore, Peters and Hurst. He describes Peters as the best player he ever worked with, and of the others he says: 'To make a good pass you need players to make themselves available for it, and people like Mooro and Geoff made it easy for me.

'People say that Mooro did not communicate enough verbally but this did not matter really because whenever you wanted to lay the ball off to him, you knew that he was always going to be available. Even when he was behind you, you could knock the ball back to him – without looking half the time – knowing that he will have anticipated it. It was the same with Geoff. One of the little sayings Ron Greenwood used in his coaching sessions was "If the space is not in front, it's behind", meaning that if there was no scope for a midfielder to hit the ball to a striker's feet, the pair of them should immediately think about a ball knocked into the space behind the defence. You could say "Well, that's simple; it's obvious." But Ron's point was that the midfielder and the striker had to be on the same wavelength mentally. Geoff was an exceptionally intelligent player, and his movement was outstanding – when it came to getting the ball to him, he made it easy for you.

'It was the same with most of the West Ham players I worked with, they were brought up to think about the game. It's what made playing for the club so enjoyable. I mean, when you've got 11 players out there all appreciating where the space is, well, then you've got a game of football.'

Knowing where the space was clearly stood Boyce in good stead when it came to getting into the box to score important goals. He only got 29 in all, but when you think of his strikes in the 1964 FA Cup semi-final and the final – and the results West Ham achieved in those matches as a consequence – who's counting?

The semi-final against Manchester United was played in driving rain and ankle-deep mud and United, with a cast of stars including Bobby Charlton, Denis Law and George Best, were hot favourites to win the trophy. Moore, having watched United's sixth-round victory at Sunderland with Johnny Byrne, was later quoted as saying: 'I don't think the semi-final hurdle is insurmountable to us – far from it. For me, United only looked a good side when they were in front. They struck me as a side who might find it very difficult to come back in a game if they were trailing by a goal or two.' The theory was put to the test as West Ham, the last team United can have expected to sit back and attempt to just contain them, raced into a 2–0 lead. The one thing that must have surprised United, though, was that the then 21-year-old Boyce, with only eight goals to his name in his previous 53 first-team matches that season (and none at all in the FA Cup), scored both of them. Those strikes, a shot from outside the box and a close-range header, did not rock United as much as Moore might have expected. Such was their comeback, especially when United had the boost of making the score 2–1, that many believe West Ham might well have eventually lost but for their 'killer' third goal. That goal, by Hurst from a Moore pass, is remembered today much more vividly than the ones that Boyce got.

But even Moore and Hurst were shoved out of the spotlight when Boyce scored the Hammers' decisive goal against Preston at Wembley. One writer, a West Ham fan, described the moment thus: 'I have seen dramatic Cup finals at Wembley. George Mutch hitting a penalty past giant Huddersfield goalkeeper Bob Hesford in the last minute of extra-time to win the match for Preston [in 1938]. The Matthews Final [between Blackpool and Bolton in 1953, when Stanley Matthews' magic helped Blackpool fight back from 3–1 down to win 4–3] . . .

'But few moments will prove as dramatic on reflection as that injury-time goal by Ronnie Boyce that proved the winner against Preston on Saturday, 2 May 1964. It was the second minute of time allowed for injuries, and West Ham were level at 2–2 with their Second Division opponents, after twice being behind. In our minds, we in the 100,000 crowd were contemplating the replay prospects and labelling the Preston wing-half, Nobby Lawton, as the man of the match.

'Then . . . Geoff Hurst, thrusting aside a lunging tackle, carried the ball forward and sent it out to the right wing to the hovering Peter Brabrook. He flighted a cunning cross over the entire Preston defence, and there, galloping in unchallenged, with the goal roar rising from the stand and terraces, was inside-right Ronnie Boyce. All eyes were riveted on the figure in the claret and light-blue shirt as he hurled himself at the ball and headed it into the net.

'All around me was ablaze with claret and light-blue scarves and favours – the Hammers had won the Cup for the first time in the club's history, in only their second FA Cup appearance at Wembley.'

Boyce has a film of the match, but says that it was only when he watched it recently that he appreciated his part in West Ham's triumph. 'I know I scored the goal, but at the time I didn't think I played that well. It's the same with a lot of players – you tend to remember the poor or average things you have done, as opposed to the good things. Outside scoring the winning goal, I really didn't think I had done anything. But when I sat down to watch it again recently, I noticed things I had forgotten about. I'm watching myself hit balls from the right side of the field to the left, make successful tackles and what have you, and I'm thinking: "Hmm . . . that weren't bad . . . That was good . . . "'

The big question, though, is did he not end up wishing he could have stood out as he did in that match more often? 'Yeah, looking back, I would like to have been more dominating. I think I could have taken the bull by the horns on certain occasions, instead of letting others do it. But I don't think I could have been any different even if I'd wanted to be. It was just my nature.'

CHAPTER 10

The Manager and Substitutes

It is difficult to imagine anybody in professional football with as much knowledge of the game as Ron Greenwood. In any university in which soccer was an academic subject, the degree course would have to be conducted by Greenwood, especially the section of it which related to the sort of individual and collective creative skill that once led the great Pele to describe football as 'The Beautiful Game'. So why is it that when looking for someone to manage the West Ham dream team, we are tempted to look beyond Greenwood and plump for John Lyall – the master's apprentice instead of the master himself? The obvious reason is that the only time that West Ham have ever truly looked capable of winning the Championship – the competition that provides the ultimate yardstick by which teams are judged – was when Lyall was in charge. Indeed, Lyall, who was a West Ham coach under Greenwood and spent three years as Greenwood's right-hand man before succeeding him as manager in 1974, brought the Hammers the best spell in the club's history. In addition to their finishing third in the Championship in 1986, his 15 years at the helm also produced two FA Cup triumphs, a Second Division Championship win (by a record 13-point margin) and an appearance in the European Cup-Winners' Cup and League Cup finals.

In terms of putting trophies in the Upton Park boardroom, Greenwood, the team manager for 13 years, did not do too badly. West Ham's European Cup-Winners' Cup win in 1965 is still regarded as their greatest achievement. Other highlights of Greenwood's reign were the team's success in winning the FA Cup in 1964 and reaching the League Cup final in 1966.

There is more than one way of assessing teams and, under Greenwood, nobody can deny that the Hammers were among the most attractive in Britain in their style of play. To anyone just wanting to see a skilful, open game of football each week – and who did not care too much about the result – West Ham's fixtures probably represented better value for money over a season than those of any other team in the country. However, when we look back on the Greenwood era, it is still difficult to dismiss the thought that his Hammers should have got their hands on more trophies than they did, especially with the advantage of having Moore, Peters and Hurst. The extent to which West Ham might have suffered through Greenwood being so much of an idealist has been a popular subject for debate by both fans and players over the years.

Moore probably put his finger on it better than anyone when Jeff Powell, his biographer, quoted him as saying: 'I couldn't deny his brilliance. The man is the encyclopedia of football. At international level, with international players, he was fantastic. In his prime without question he would have made a tremendous England manager. Perhaps an even better manager of England than Alf Ramsey. Even when his chance came late, giving England stability after Don Revie went off to the desert, he was in his element. He lost Kevin Keegan and Trevor Brooking yet still came home from the 1982 World Cup finals in Spain undefeated. On a World Cup level, everybody in the England squad understood him and benefited from him.

'Ron has been involved in every FIFA report and analysis that has mattered. He sees things in football that are beyond the comprehension of many players and coaches in the game. That was one of his problems at West Ham. Ron talked about the game at such a high level that sometimes it went straight over the head of the average player. Some days, I believe there were only a couple of us who understood a word he was on about. He never seemed to realise that he should be talking down to half the team. I was the one who was always being falsely accused of not adjusting to the need to play bread-and-butter club football. Yet really, Ron was the one who needed to work with the best, the élite players.'

One apparent anomaly in all this was that Moore, and other players who became international stars under Greenwood, was not in the élite category when the manager first started working with them. Indeed, it is possible that some of them never would have been but for Greenwood's coaching skills and appreciation of how they could best be deployed. There are few players who worked under Greenwood – if any – who do not readily concede that they became better players as a result of the experience.

Greenwood did not appear to have been talking over players' heads at half-time in the 1964 FA Cup final against Preston. The Hammers were 2–1 down, but thanks to Greenwood's team-talk and the tactical changes he initiated, they went on to win 3–2.

Greenwood recalled: 'I felt we were giving Preston too much time and room in midfield, and that our set-up wasn't right for the dual threat of Alex Dawson and Alec Ashworth. They were making good use of the big pitch and Moore was being by-passed. He was doing nothing. My answer was to play squarer at the back than I'd have liked, with Moore shifting up alongside Brown to mark Preston's two strikers and to push Bovington forward to make earlier impact. In short, we reversed our tactics, and it worked.'

This was by no means an isolated example of Greenwood's tactical expertise, but Moore's view does make sense of Lyall's success afterwards because Lyall could be said to have taken on the role of Greenwood's interpreter. He had learned much from Greenwood, and was able to edit those lessons and then present them in a more pragmatic and practical form. In his book, Lyall, referring to his early days as a coach of a local amateur side, unwittingly brought us back to Moore's view of Greenwood when he said: 'All I did in those days was imitate the training routines we used at West Ham. But it was sometimes frustrating trying to coach players at a lower level to achieve the skills and fitness of the professionals at Upton Park. It was a big lesson for me, and I soon realised that I had to tailor my coaching sessions to the level of the players I was dealing with.' He was shrewd enough to take the best of Greenwood and combine it with his own ideas and methods. Hence the fact that, under his command, West Ham continued to play good football – but were stronger physically and better organised in defence. They were better balanced.

Lyall, whose own West Ham playing career as a full-back was cut short by injury after just 34 first-team games, and who spent a total of 34 years on the Upton Park staff, had much in common with Greenwood. He had the same sense of personal integrity, the same sense of responsibility towards his players as both people and professionals. 'Our relationship was a very good one,' Greenwood has said. 'John is a strong character with a Scottish background, stable, straight and single-minded. He has a nice, easy manner and I discovered very quickly that he was a person after my own heart. He wanted to know every-thing about the job, but more than that, he cared passionately about the game. He was also a family man, who cared about people for their own sake.'

In the modern game, one suspects that Greenwood and Lyall (who once described Greenwood as being 'a constant source of inspiration to me') would have dovetailed perfectly in the respective club roles of director of football and first-team coach. In fact, they did establish a similar relationship when Lyall took over from Greenwood as manager and Greenwood became West Ham's general manager. Greenwood held the post for three seasons before leaving to become England manager; and, as if to emphasise the advantages of Lyall and Greenwood continuing to work together, it was in the first of those three seasons – the 1974–75 campaign – that West Ham won the FA Cup again.

The most memorable aspects of that triumph, of course, were that the Fulham team the Hammers beat in the final included Bobby Moore and that both the Hammers' goals in the 2–0 Wembley win came from a then relatively unknown striker by the name of Alan Taylor. Taylor's presence reflected considerable credit on Lyall, not to mention Greenwood, who recommended that the club buy the youngster from Rochdale for £40,000 the previous November. By the time the Hammers were due to face Arsenal in the FA Cup quarter-final at Highbury, Taylor had made only three first-team appearances, two as substitute. But Lyall decided to take the gamble of playing him against Arsenal instead of the more experienced Bobby Gould, because he felt Taylor's pace might cause problems to the Gunners on the left side of their defence. Taylor scored two goals that day and, with Lyall electing to keep him in the side, he repaid the manager again with two goals in the 2–1 semi-final replay victory over Ipswich at Villa Park.

As for the final, Lyall's ability to come up with a winning formula was also seen in the limited scope Moore and his fellow veteran central defender Alan Mullery were given to settle on the ball and dictate the play for Fulham from the back, and the selection of Patsy Holland wide on the left because of his ability to produce crosses that would curl away from Moore. Lyall showed an even more impressive degree of expertise in the 1985 final, when the then Second Division Hammers beat Arsenal 1–0 with that rare headed goal by Trevor Brooking.

Lyall tells it like this: 'Eddie Bailey [West Ham's chief scout] and I had watched Arsenal twice and had devised a plan that we believed would cause them a little concern. Arsenal had a well-balanced team and a rigid defensive pattern. I felt we needed to come up with something a little different, something that would confuse them and perhaps disturb their defensive organisation. I decided to play David Cross as a lone striker and drop his attacking partner, Stuart Pearson, into a withdrawn position in front of the midfield. Cross was such a willing and resilient striker that we felt he had the strength to occupy both the Arsenal centre-backs, O'Leary and Young. In theory, they should have been able to mark Dave successfully between them, but what they wouldn't be so sure about was how to mark Stuart Pearson. He played in the hole between Dave and our midfield. Arsenal had to decide whether to mark him with a defender or a midfield player. Whatever they did, it would disrupt their pattern. Alternatively, they could leave him free to play unhindered. It worked out exceptionally well for us. Arsenal never really solved the problem.'

The Hammers took full advantage of their opponents' discomfort at a time when it was at its most pronounced, with Brooking scoring his goal after 13 minutes. At half-time, Lyall set the Gunners another problem. 'I told the players that Arsenal might now push either Young or O'Leary forward to mark Pearson. If they did that, I told them, we would simply play the ball straight to David Cross, who would then be playing one-on-one.'

With an XI like this comprising the West Ham fantasy team, half of whose members became managers or coaches themselves, some might say that the need for a Lyall and a Greenwood is far from obvious. But having such a pair in charge of this lot would surely be the icing on the cake, especially when you consider the high number of players who would not be struggling to stop Greenwood's unrivalled pearls of football wisdom from going over their heads.

＊　　　＊　　　＊

We've got the starting line-up. We've got the right management team to bring the best out of them and help them wipe the floor with the opposition in the way that only an on-song West Ham XI can. But what about the substitutes to enable Greenwood and Lyall to change the shape of their side, or give the likes of Moore, Peters and Hurst a rest when they have become bored by having too much of the ball? If one accepts that the dream team does not need another specialist goalkeeper – Peters could handle that role, just as he did all the others he was given – how about a subs' bench with the backsides of Frank Lampard, Ken Brown, Harry Redknapp, Johnny Byrne and Frank McAvennie on it?

Brown and Byrne have to be included in the squad if only for their sense of humour and easy-going, affable personalities. Never in the Hammers' history has there been two more like-able, popular blokes in the dressing-room than Brown and

Byrne. That's not the only reason why their claims for inclusion are so strong. Byrne was arguably the most talented of all West Ham centre-forwards, as Greenwood indicated when describing him as the 'English Di Stefano'. The ever-amiable, ever-smiling Brown was a centre-half who could be placed at the other end of the English football scale – a straightforward, traditional stopper who focused his attention on his basic ball-winning responsibilities and, unlike Moore, Alvin Martin and Rio Ferdinand, looked upon the space outside his penalty area almost as forbidden territory.

In a team like West Ham, it is always useful to have one or two people like Brown, who relish staying close to their goal and minding the shop. It is also useful to have someone who can take on the responsibility of keeping an eye on the irrepressible Byrne, a man whose conduct could be somewhat unorthodox, if not outrageous. When Byrne was at West Ham that responsibility fell mainly to Brown, who had the dubious privilege of sharing a room with him. It would be stretching a point to say that Brown was his 'minder'. Nonetheless, West Ham clearly felt that if anyone was going to have a steadying influence on the number 9, it was going to be their solid, dependable centre-half.

In any event, Brown was a good listener, which was a particularly handy quality when you had to listen to Byrne's non-stop patter. Not for nothing was Byrne nicknamed 'Budgie'.

Greenwood signed Johnny Byrne from Crystal Palace for a then club record fee of £58,000, plus forward Ronnie Brett in March 1962, and had no hesitation in describing him as a centre-forward 'who had everything'. That was some praise, given Greenwood's standards, but nobody felt that it was an exaggeration. Byrne struck the perfect balance between individualism and team play. Quick and imaginative, his first touch, his control in both dribbling and passing did much to bring out the best in Geoff Hurst as a striker. Indeed, Greenwood felt that when Budgie was on song up front, West Ham were on song as a team. One of his greatest attributes was his ability to receive the ball with his back to the opposing goal and either spin around his marker or set up a scoring chance for someone else. It was this aspect of his game which created the Leeds United nightmare of that remarkable 7–0 thrashing by West Ham in the League Cup tie at Upton Park in November 1966.

He was no less interesting as a person. Greenwood described him as a 'delightful character, all chat and humour'. The manager recalled that when he once visited Byrne in a Catholic hospital, he was taken aback to find the nuns running around in circles for him and even putting his bets on for him. 'Budgie was everybody's friend, but in a way he was his own worst enemy. I told him early on that he should play for England past 30, but he was not a moderate man. He couldn't say no. He lived his life to the limit.' One occasion on which this proved particularly disturbing to West Ham was when Byrne, having damaged a knee playing for England against Scotland in 1965 (which kept him out of the European Cup-Winners' Cup final), was allowed to accompany his colleagues to the United States for a close-season tournament in New York. Byrne joined some of the other players at a German beer garden at a World Fair in the city, and though still not fully recovered from his injury, thought nothing of attempting to give an example of his gymnastic ability by jumping on and off a stagecoach. He eventually fell off and injured the knee again.

Mention Byrne's name to Ken Brown and he shakes his head and rolls his eyes. He says: 'Oh blimey, Ron Greenwood had a difficult player to handle in Johnny Byrne. Bloody hell. I remember Ron saying to me "Look, we've just signed Johnny Byrne and I want you to be his room-mate because I think you'll be a good influence on him." The bloody headaches that caused me. But I thought the little fellow was brilliant, he could really play and was tremendous fun to be with – and we became the closest of friends.'

Not that there weren't occasions that the friendship could have been deemed to be in jeopardy. Brown recalls a match at Fulham, when he was team captain in the absence of the injured Moore.

'In the dressing-room, I said: "Right lads, out we go," and off

I went on to the field with the ball under my arm. But when I looked around, there was no one there, nobody was following me. Budgie had held them all back, hadn't he? "Let him go out on his own," he said. I felt a right twit.

'That was Budgie, always up to mischief. You couldn't go to sleep too often with him around. You know, if he were sitting here now, he'd be tapping his foot and thinking: "What can I do now?" He was hyperactive, a bit like Paul Gascoigne is said to be. I remember waking up on the day of the FA Cup semi-final against Manchester United at Hillsborough, and Budgie saying to me: "We won't play this match today – it hasn't stopped raining all night." I said: "How do you know? You've been asleep." But he hadn't – believe it or not, he had been up all night.

'The person I felt sorry for was his wife, Margaret. I think it helped put her mind at ease when she knew he was with me. We used to joke about it. She used to say to me "I love you – if I dump him, will you marry me?"

'Up to everything, Budgie was. We were in Ghana, our room was on the top floor of the hotel and the rain was coming down in buckets. Anyway, we looked out of the window and saw these little kiddies in the playground, which was ankle-deep in mud. Budgie says to me: "Hey, give us some coins." So I gave him some coins, and the next thing you knew, he has thrown them out of the window and all the little kids have dived into the mud to get them. There was mud everywhere, all the kids were absolutely covered in mud looking for the coins. They loved it and so did he. It set him off, didn't it? He had to do some more.

'Our hotel had a circular staircase, and when you looked down it, from the floor our room was on, you could actually see the ground floor. One night, when we were heading back to our rooms after a match, we got to the top of the stairs and Budgie, who had a bottle of beer, said: "Do you think I could get this bottle down to the bottom without it hitting the side rail?" I said: "Don't even think about it, don't be stupid." He said he had to do it. I said: "You can't." He said: "No, I am going to do it." So he dropped the bottle, and I think it must have hit everything going down. It was clatter, clatter, clatter – and then you heard the sound of it smashing to pieces as it hit the ground. At that, Budgie has just run off, hasn't he?

'The next morning, Ron's got us all together and he says: "I'm not a very happy person. Someone's been misbehaving and we're not leaving this room until that person has owned up." Budgie stood up and admitted: "It was me – sorry, guv," and I remember Ron just looking at him knowingly and saying "Oh, I might have guessed . . . I might have guessed it was you."

'I'm not sure how long Budgie would have survived at West Ham had it not been for Ron. Not a lot of managers would have put up with him, but Ron would always forgive him somewhere down the line.'

This was something that all of Byrne's West Ham team-mates applauded – and none more so than Brown. 'Ron understood Budgie and knew what made him tick,' he says. 'Budgie was a great, great footballer, and as a person, well, you couldn't help loving him.'

Many would say that about Ken Brown, too.

The choices of Moore, Peters and Hurst as the first players to take their places in the West Ham dream team dressing-room are obvious. To those who believe in the importance of teams having players with the right personalities, it is equally appropriate that some space also be found there for Brown before the door is closed.

Brown, who was a West Ham player for 15 seasons between 1952 and 1967 and made 455 first-team appearances, readily concedes that he did not have the skill that hallmarked so many of his team-mates. So much so that his reaction to being included in a group of central defenders like Moore, Martin and Ferdinand is one of amazement. But leaving aside the question of how much he is inclined to underestimate himself, there were other areas in which he stood out. One of the most significant of these was that Brown, open and friendly and with a penchant for never taking himself too seriously, was one of the West Ham stars who have best epitomised the spirit of the club.

West Ham have long had a tradition as a warm, loyal, closely-knit club – a club reflecting all the beloved characteristics of the working-class east-end Cockney public in which their large support-base is rooted. There are no airs and graces about West Ham FC, nor the vast majority of the men who have been employed by them. If any Premiership club can be described as a people's club, in these days of mega TV deals, corporate hospitality and merchandising, it is West Ham.

Brown, born and bred in Dagenham in the same road as Terry Venables and Les Allen, has summed up that image perfectly. He was a player with whom the fans could easily identify. He had to sweat and toil for his money just as they did, and never lost sight of the sort of life he might have had but for his 'good fortune' in becoming a professional footballer. As he says, 'My father was a furniture-maker, and he took me into the business when I left school at 15. We used to have some beautiful warm, sunny days, but for two years I'd be working under this blooming glass roof learning to be a wood-machinist.' In terms of his attitude and his personality, the fans looked upon him as one of them. With that self-deprecating sense of humour and engaging, easy-going nature, he was no less popular among his West Ham colleagues. Even now, being in the company of Brown – a director of the Lakenham Leisure Centre in Norwich – is an uplifting experience. He laughs a lot, especially at himself, and you quickly realise why those who were part of the West Ham dressing-room scene when he was around got so much enjoyment from his presence.

The players who were at West Ham at the time Brown joined the club at 17 in 1951 will certainly have got a lot of enjoyment from the teenager's relationship with the Hammers' veteran centre-half, Dick Walker. The latter, then in his late 30s and approaching the end of his long Upton Park career, lived close to Brown and was encouraged by the manager, Ted Fenton, to take him under his wing.

'Dick was my mentor, he more or less gave me my education in professional football. But what a character.

'The first day I met him, he said: "Right, we'll get the bus [to the ground] each morning, so you be at my place at nine o'clock." So the first morning, I got there at about five to nine, and when he opened the door, he said: "What time is it?" I told him it was about two minutes to nine, and he said: "I told you nine", and with that he slammed the door. The following day I got there at a minute past nine and found him standing outside going mad. "You're never going to get it right, are you?" he said.'

Walker then suggested that he and Brown should take it in turns to pay the bus fare each day – and also for the tea at the café they visited before the start of training. 'But Dick didn't have to pay anything,' Brown says. 'He was very friendly with one of the conductresses on that bus route, and when it was his turn to pay the fares, he would insist on catching her bus, knowing that she wouldn't take any money from him. Because he was so well known – he'd been a West Ham star since before the war – he got the tea free of charge, too.' But, as far as Walker was concerned, this did not mean that Brown should change his part of the 'pact'.

'We get on the bus,' Brown recalls, 'and he says, "Get the fare." I said, "Hang on a minute – you didn't get the fare yesterday." At this, Dick told me to repeat what we had agreed, that I would get the fare one day and he would get it the next, and then he said: "You got it Monday, and it was my turn on Tuesday. It's Wednesday now – get the fare."' Many in Brown's position would have got the needle. But that was not the way he was made. 'Oh, Dick was brilliant. I loved the guy.'

On the field, too, Brown gave the impression of not having one ounce of malice in his whole body. The only time he can ever recall losing his temper during a match was when the Northern Ireland centre-forward, Derek Dougan, 'took the piss' out of him when scoring a hat-trick against him for Blackburn at Ewood Park.

Brown explains: 'After each goal Dougan turned around, pointed at me and went "Ha, ha, ha." Andy Malcolm [the Hammers' tough-tackling wing-half] was a great buddy of mine and he said: "Don't worry – we'll have him when he comes down to our place." I was saying, "Oh yeah, I'll make sure I have the last laugh", but really I knew that there was no way I could kick him deliberately. No matter how fired up I was, I knew I couldn't do it.'

But Malcolm could. As it turned out, it wasn't until two or three seasons later that Dougan appeared in a match at Upton Park, and it says much about the affection for Brown among his West Ham colleagues that even by that time Malcolm was still in no mood to allow Dougan to get away with his arrogance. 'Dougan was going down the inside-left channel and Andy was trundling after him,' Brown explains. 'Then, as Dougan got to the by-line and was about to cross the ball, Andy just went *crunch* – he just trampled all over him and sent him crashing into the advertising hoardings behind the goal.'

Brown himself got his first experience of going through the pain barrier in the 1952–53 season, when he came into the team for the first time (for three matches) because of injuries to Walker and Malcolm Allison. In a game against Birmingham – only the second league game of his career – he was caught in the face by a full-blooded shot by centre-forward Tommy Briggs, causing him to fall to the ground like a sack of coal. 'My mum was there and she cried her eyes out,' Brown says. 'She thought I was dead.'

Another reason why Brown has vivid memories of that period in his career concerns his fondness for another of those great West Ham 'characters', goalkeeper Ernie Gregory: 'We were playing at Rotherham, and about five minutes from the end, with the score at 0–0, they were awarded a penalty. The fellow hit it perfectly – it looked a certain goal – but big Ernie somehow managed to get across to the ball and keep it out. I don't think I have ever been more excited in my whole life. I rushed up to him and put my arms around him, I was almost dragging him off his feet. He then got really agitated. "Stop it – stop it, will you? Just control yourself," he shouted. "What's up, Ernie?" I said. "Sod it," he replied. "I should have held that penalty."'

Brown, of course, was also a character himself, which helps explain why the West Ham crowd were so fond of him: 'When I went on to the park, I used to have a habit of sprinting right across to the chicken run, just to get any tension out of my system, and because I did it so regularly I built up a little rapport with some of the spectators there. One day, I'm warming up and I hear someone shout, "Hey, Brownie," and when I looked over, there was a black guy there. "All right, boy?" he asked. I nodded and waved to him, and from then on it became a ritual – every home game, he would be standing on the same spot and we'd have this little exchange. The other lads said he must like me because of my name, so it was quite funny when I gave him a wave before one match and he shouted: "Can't be on your side today, boy." We were playing Blackburn.'

Brown can entertain you for hours with such anecdotes. But there is a serious side to him as well, especially when he talks about his sense of insecurity when playing for West Ham under Greenwood. Insecurity? Brown did a wonderful job for the club in the 1957–58 season, when he gained a regular first-team place as a result of Malcolm Allison's career being cruelly destroyed through tuberculosis, and steered the club to promotion to the First Division. His impact was such that the following year he got into the England team against Northern Ireland. Among the other highlights of his long reign at the heart of the Hammers' defence were his solid displays alongside Bobby Moore in the 1964 FA Cup and 1965 European Cup-Winners' Cup triumphs. But for all that, Brown still feels he was fortunate to survive at Upton Park under Greenwood's management.

He says: 'I idolised Ron, but I never ever thought that Ron fancied me as a player. I don't think I could ever do enough to satisfy him – I don't, honestly. He even had me in tears at times, believe me.

'Ron was a perfectionist, perhaps too much of a perfectionist because in my view no team can work properly with 11 world-class players. You've got to have a rough diamond in there somewhere. The big problem for me was that I played with Bobby Moore, and I always had the impression that Ron would look at me and think: "Why can't you do what he can do?" As a centre-half himself, Ron wanted to put his foot on the ball and stroke it about, so he'd have probably preferred to have someone like that in his team, rather than me. I know for a fact that he made enquiries about other centre-halfs. One I know he liked was Tony Knapp [the former Southampton and England player].'

It is possible, of course, that Greenwood deliberately encouraged such thoughts, a point that Brown makes himself when referring to West Ham's 2–1 win over Spain's Real Zaragoza in the 1965 European Cup-Winners' Cup semi-final first leg at Upton Park.

'Before the game, Ron said: "Look, I don't want you to go near their centre-forward – in the air, he's the best continental striker I have seen for years. He's not the tallest of people, but he's just fabulous in the air." Even as we were about to take the field, Ron says: "Don't forget – stay away from him when the ball's in the air because he'll leave you for dead." But the first high ball that came into the middle, I thought: "I know I can win this ball, I know I can." It was my natural instinct to go for it, and I did. I really had no problem at all in pumping it clear and the other fellow was nowhere near me. I'm thinking: "Where is he, then?" You know, throughout the whole game, he did not give me any trouble at all. I don't know why Ron said he was so worried about the guy. The only reason I can think of is that he said it to wind me up and keep me on my toes.'

Not that it matters. Brown would be more than happy to work with Greenwood again in the West Ham dream team. 'As I said, I idolised the fellow. I mean, when I see him now, I hug him. He's lovely.'